Law, Immunization and the Right to Die

Law, Immunization and the Right to Die focuses on the urgent matter of legal appeals and judicial decisions on assisted death. Drawing on key cases from the United Kingdom and Canada, the book focuses on the problematic paternalism of legal decisions that currently deny assisted dying and questions why the law fails to recognize what many describe as "compassionate motives" for assisted death. When cases are analyzed as discourses that are part of a larger socio-political logic of governance, judicial decisions reveal themselves as relying on the construction of neoliberal fictions—fictions that are here elucidated with reference to Michel Foucault's theoretical insights on pastoral power and Roberto Esposito's philosophical thesis on immunization.

Challenging the socio-political logic of neoliberalism, the issue of assisted dying goes beyond the predominant legal concern with protecting—or immunizing—individuals from one another, in favor of minimal interference. This book calls for a new kind of politics: one that might affirm people and their finitude both more collectively and more compassionately.

Jennifer Hardes is a Lecturer in Education at Canterbury Christ Church University, UK. Her research examines how legal and medical expert knowledge is constructed and interpreted to make judicial, medical and broader governmental decisions, particularly regarding policies and laws on health and medical-related issues.

Law, Immunization and the Right to Die

Jennifer Hardes

Routledge
Taylor & Francis Group
LONDON AND NEW YORK

First published 2016
by Routledge

2 Park Square, Milton Park, Abingdon, Oxfordshire OX14 4RN
711 Third Avenue, New York, NY 10017

a GlassHouse book

Routledge is an imprint of the Taylor & Francis Group, an informa business

First issued in paperback 2017

British Library Cataloguing in Publication Data
A catalogue record for this book is available from the British Library

Library of Congress Cataloging-in-Publication Data
Hardes, Jennifer.
Law, immunization and the right to die / Jennifer Hardes.
pages cm
Includes bibliographical references and index.
ISBN 978-1-138-94320-9 (hbk) — ISBN 978-1-315-67265-6 (ebk)
1. Right to die—Law and legislation. 2. Right to die—Philosophy.
3. Euthanasia—Social aspects. 4. Autonomy (Psychology) I. Title.
K3611.E95H37 2016
344.04'197—dc23
2015036561

ISBN: 978-1-138-94320-9 (hbk)
ISBN: 978-1-138-57039-9 (pbk)

Typeset in Baskerville by
by FiSH Books Ltd, Enfield

Contents

Acknowledgements

I would like to thank the following friends and colleagues for their thoughtful contributions, feedback, and support in writing this book: George Pavlich, Catherine Kellogg, Bryan Hogeveen, Judy Davidson, Kate Davies, Sean Ryan and Judy Liao. Thank you to the Sociology Department at the University of Alberta and the Faculty of Education at Canterbury Christ Church University for the funding and time that supported the writing of the book. Thank you also to the editorial team at Routledge, particularly Laura Muir and Colin Perrin. Finally it goes without saying that my biggest thanks are to John and Sarah Hardes.

Table of Cases

Introduction

Immunized Life

"Whose body is this? Who owns my life?" Canada's Sue Rodriguez demanded an answer to these stark questions as she engaged in what has now become known as a landmark legal battle in cases colloquially dubbed 'the right to die' (*Rodriguez v British Columbia* (Attorney General) [1993] 3 S.C.R. 519; *Rodriguez v British Columbia* (Attorney General), [1993] CanLII 1191 (BC CA)). Rodriguez was diagnosed in August 1991 with amyotrophic lateral sclerosis (ALS), also commonly known as motor neurone disease. ALS is a debilitating and degenerative illness that weakens the muscles and eventually leads of a loss of bodily movement. Realizing that this malady would eventually leave her unable to move and entirely dependent on others, Rodriguez felt that she was left with two decisions: she could either end her life legally by way of suicide, which was decriminalized in Canada in 1972, or she could await a time at which she would be unable to end her life herself and thus risk living a life "trapped in her own body" given that at this late stage it would be illegal for another person to provide her assistance in dying. For her, the prospect of a life confined to a body that she could not move was unfathomable. Yet, after a tedious wait for what the courts called "careful consideration," Rodriguez's "right" to die was refused.

Over three decades later, Canada's courts witnessed a similar appeal from Gloria Taylor, who was diagnosed with ALS in 2009. Faced with what did not seem like much by way of a choice, Taylor took to the British Columbia Court of Appeal in 2012 to fight in much the same way as Rodriguez had done so for the "right to die" (*Carter v Canada* (Attorney General) [2012] BCSC 886). She wanted assurance that when the time came, and when she finally reached the later stages of her illness that would leave physically incapable of ending her own life, she could have the help of another person to end her suffering. While those opposed to a change in law argued that the decision in *Rodriguez* set a precedent and that the courts were bound by *stare decisis*, the ruling judge in Taylor's case, Justice Lynn Smith, commenced with what was to become a landmark case for Canada: Smith granted Taylor a constitutional exemption that would allow her the right to assisted death and gave parliament one year to decide how to respond. Celebrations followed; however, they were short lived. The decision was later overturned by a higher court in 2013, rendering Smith's decision void (*Carter v Canada* (Attorney General) [2013] BCCA 435). Sadly in the meantime Taylor passed away, unable to see her case take further course of action. Despite taking some time to gain traction, the earlier dismissal of appeal was later overturned once again by the Canadian Supreme Court. In 2015, weighed by various factors, Canada's highest court decided that assisted dying ought to be rendered legal and Canada's parliament was once again given a year to articulate its response to this matter.

Almost in tandem to Taylor's case but on the other side of the Atlantic, England witnessed the emotionally charged appeal from 58-year-old Tony Nicklinson, a formerly active man who, after experiencing a stroke in 2005, was left paralyzed from the neck downward. He described his remaining life as his own "personal purgatory", trapped, as Rodriguez and Taylor had also noted, between life and death. Indeed as Nicklinson's daughter, Lauren, noted: "If a prisoner were held in these conditions in a prison, there would rightly be accusations of torture. Dad's prison was of a wholly more tortuous nature."[1] "If the legal consequences were not so huge i.e. life imprisonment, perhaps I could get someone to help me," commented Nicklinson: "As things stand, I can't get help" (*R (Nicklinson) v Ministry of Justice* [2012] EWHC 2381 (Admin), (2012) MHLO 77, paragraph 3). Despite a series of appeals between 2012 and 2014 from Nicklinson and from his wife, Jane, asking the law for the right to allow a physician to help end his life compassionately, Nicklinson's legal case was denied. The English law could not allow the prospect of "compassionate killing" from a physician or from any other subject: the law simply did not recognize the "compassionate motives of the 'mercy' killer" (*Nicklinson v MOJ*, paragraph 54, s7.7).

These appeals from Rodriguez, Taylor and Nicklinson—amongst various others—are most broadly considered appeals to "assisted death." Acts of assistance in death differ: one may appeal for a physician to administer a lethal injection in order to end one's life, which is termed "voluntary active euthanasia;"[2] on the contrary assisted death can also be interpreted and sought as "assisted suicide," whereby a physician provides the appellant with the means to administer his or her own death. With assisted suicide the doctor will not physically inject the subject or administer a lethal dose, but instead will provide the means for the subject to do so themselves (Lemmens and Dickens, 2001). When I refer to "right to die" legal appeals throughout, I refer to a group of legal appeals that emerged in the 1970s (Lavi, 2008) that have asked the law to respond to the prospect of assisted dying practices more broadly, including appeals to voluntary active euthanasia as well as assisted suicide. I often use the terms "right to die" and "assisted dying/death appeals" interchangeably.

Earlier appeals to the "right to die" also encompassed other acts of assistance—or, as the law will claim, encompassed other "omissions"—that have since been legalized, including practices of palliative sedation and passive euthanasia. The former, also sometimes called "terminal sedation," refers to the use of medications that induce an unconscious state; its aim is to "relieve the burden of otherwise intractable suffering in a manner that is ethically acceptable to the patient, family and health-care providers" in imminently dying patients (Cherny and Radbruch, 2009: 581). Palliative sedation has long been a medical practice, with no legislation having directly addressed it and with no court cases that have directly tested it as a practice in England and Canada (Dean *et al.*, 2012). The latter, passive euthanasia, is defined as the removal or withdrawal of life sustaining treatment, which includes turning off a respirator or removing a subject's artificial nutrition (Garrard and Wilkinson, 2005). Practices of passive euthanasia were set as a precedent in England in the 1993 case of *Airedale NHS Trust v Bland* [1993] AC 789. In Canada, in 1992, the case of *Nancy B. v Hotel-Dieu de Quebec* [1992], 86 D.L.R. (4th) 385 (Que. S.C.) dealt with a passive euthanasia case, but it did not set a precedent because it was decided in a first-instance court (the judge's decision was not appealed), despite being cited in the later 'active' *Rodriguez* case. The legalization of some of these acts, the manner of overlooking others, and the continued denial of other acts still, has been a source of controversy for appellants and for scholars writing on this topic area (e.g., Lemmens and Dickens, 2001; Tännsjö, 2004).

Despite the increased popularity of appeals to assisted death that have continued to make news headlines in various countries, only three places in the world have open legislation regarding the prospect of "voluntary active euthanasia": the Netherlands, since 2002; Belgium, since 2002; and Luxembourg, since 2009. Other countries have opened legislation that allows "assisted suicide," including: Switzerland, since 1941; and the United States (Oregon since 1997; Washington since

2008; Montana since 2008; Vermont since 2013; and New Mexico since 2014). Some countries do not have specific laws regarding assisted suicide and euthanasia but may "prosecute such cases under other legislation" (Yuill, 2013: 22) (e.g., Sweden, Finland, Germany, Denmark, Uruguay). Thus, the legal treatment of the act differs between these countries. For example, in Sweden, law treats assisted suicide as manslaughter (Humphry, 2005; Yuill, 2013). Other countries have also recently been pulled into the debate; for instance, a recent Irish legal case challenged the law's denial of assisted suicide and voluntary active euthanasia (*Fleming v Ireland* IESC 19 [2013]. Likewise, toward the end of 2013 a French couple, Georgette and Bernard Cazes, aged 86, made news headlines for engaging in a double suicide in a hotel, leaving a letter appealing for the right to assisted dying and the prospect of "dignified death" that has since stirred assisted dying debates in France. In response, President François Hollande set in motion a recommendation to legalize assisted suicide that was part of his pre-election pledge. The Scottish parliament also recently (2015) voted to reject legislation on assisted dying. Even countries that legalized practices of assisted dying some time ago such as Belgium have recently reopened debates to extend the prospects of assisted dying to children; the Belgium senate voted to legalize this act in December of 2013, which Parliament passed in March of 2014.

In Canada, which forms part of the focus of this book, we have already heard of the landmark case in 2015 that has set a new precedent regarding the right to assisted death. Prior to that, Canada was engaged in discussions concerning Bill 52 *An Act Respecting End of Life Care*, which was tabled in Quebec in June 2013. Bill 52, which was considered dead after dissolution of the National Assembly when Quebec Premier Pauline Marois called for a new election, was debated and passed on June 5th 2014. This has been referred to as "right to die" legislation, though it specifically claims to provide "end of life palliative care" for those who are deemed terminally ill under a series of carefully crafted provisions. Bill 52 does not formally claim to permit voluntary active euthanasia or assisted suicide per se, both of which prior to the landmark *Carter v Canada* (Attorney General), 2015 SCC 5, [2015] 1 S.C.R. 331 ruling were not permitted by federal government and were claimed to be contra to the Canadian Criminal Code.

In England, which also forms the focus of this book, the law has not been so lenient. The courts have thus far consistently decided that voluntary active euthanasia and physician-assisted suicide is to remain unlawful: there can be no "right to die." While suicide was decriminalized in 1961 and in the 1990s a precedent was set in *Bland* that legalized "passive" euthanasia, the law still denies what it regards as "active" forms of assistance. This matter was most recently concluded in 2014 in a Supreme Court ruling on the case of *R (Nicklinson & Lamb) v Ministry of Justice, R (AM) v Director of Public* Prosecutions [2014] UKSC 38 25 June 2014. The court, led by Lord Neuberger, heard an appeal from Nicklinson, whose previous appeals had been denied, in association with Paul Lamb, another right to die appellant, alongside "Martin," who sought clarity as to whether a care worker could assist with travel to Dignitas without fear of prosecution. The decision followed precedent set in a swell of earlier debates concerning the right to die that emerged in the early 2000s: Dianne Pretty's appeal to physician-assisted death was denied in the early 2000s by both the English courts and on appeal to the European Court of Human Rights (see *R (Pretty) v Director of Public Prosecutions* [2001] UKHL 61; *Pretty v The United Kingdom* [2002] ECHR 427). However, there were also "grey areas" regarding assisted death that were explored and, when appealed, clarified and permitted. Such was the case of *R (Purdy) v Director of Public Prosecutions* [2009] EWCA Civ 92; *R (Purdy) v Director of Public Prosecutions* [2010] 1 AC 345 that led to the issuing of a 2010 policy document in which the Director of Public Prosecutions (DPP) outlined terms associated with likelihood of prosecution regarding those who would assist loved ones to travel to a destination where assisted death is legal without fear of prosecution in one's home country. Some continue to regard this 2010 policy as unclear on certain matters; for example, Martin's appeal in 2014 asked for clarity from the DPP regarding the likelihood that "strangers" such as care workers would be able to assist in travel to Dignitas. This appeal was, however, denied and it was noted that there was no reason to order the DPP to conduct a review based on Martin's appeal. Rather it was noted in the case that "she [the DPP] will no doubt be considering this position in light of the decisions made in this Court and in the Court of Appeal" (*R (Nicklinson & Lamb) v Ministry of Justice, R (AM) v Director of Public Prosecutions* [2014] UKSC 38 25 June 2014, paragraph 323). As Lord Neuberger noted in this case, even without absolute clarity in the law regarding the likelihood of prosecution, before the case of *Purdy* from which the 2010 policy emerged, between 1998 and 2011, 215 British people travelled to Dignitas and none of those assisting this travel were prosecuted. Indeed, it is said that as many as a quarter of suicide cases at Dignitas, a well-known assisted-suicide clinic in Switzerland, are British: some are calling this "suicide tourism" (Gauthier *et al.*, 2014).

While "progression" was allegedly made with some forms of assistance in death according to right to die advocates, the law continues to refuse what it has framed as "acts" of assistance that involve taking the life of another person or "actively" providing the means for this person to take their own life. Those who favor assisted dying view the English law as archaic: it does not keep up with the times. Many also regard it as a cruel injustice imposed on vulnerable persons. Given the recent waves of appeals to the law to open up its prospects for assisted suicide and active euthanasia, scholar Thomas Tierney's (2006) earlier comment has proven to be even more pertinent: of all the bioethical dilemmas to have emerged in the 21st century the "right to die" has truly become one of the most "visible and divisive."

These reflections on the current state of law and its decisions on forms of assisted dying spurs a series of significant questions regarding law and its logic: why does the law allow some forms of death but refuse others and impose what subjects regard as a tyrannical "life sentence?" Why does this life sentence seem to be inflicted on particular kinds of subjects who are typically categorized as "vulnerable?" And why does the law declare as illegal the act of assisting a subject with his or her death when this subject has requested such death and when the assistance is framed as a benevolent act? Whilst the law claims it is precisely *because* it is compassionate that it acts with such perceived cruelty, advocates of the right to die continue to condemn the English law as cruel and lacking in compassion. It seems that compassion and cruelty are two sides of the same legal coin: a benevolent law "protects" its subjects, but in doing so such a law also causes pain and suffering to these very subjects. It is this relation between suffering and protection that I turn to next.

Immunization and Assisted Death

One might wonder what immunization has to do with assisted death. Besides both being "medical" terms, immunization and assisted death seem to share little-to-nothing in common. Immunization refers to a defense against disease and infection or biological invasion. An immune response kicks in when our body is presented with an alien or foreign object—a "non-self"—an "immunogen;" our immune system helps fight this agent and fortify us against it. Yet immunization is not only a medical concept. In politics we use also the term "immunity," this time to refer to political exemption or a form of safe passage: immunity is a protection from prosecution (Esposito, 2008, 2010).

In both medical and political instances, immunization is used to explain a mode of shutting out and closing off; immunity operates to defend and protect a subject. It is this common point that both medical and political forms of immunization share that forms the uptake of immunization in this book. It is the focus on closure around the self—the "protection" from what exists on the "outside"—that makes immunization such a helpful concept to explain the issue of assisted dying which is also, at once, both a medical and a political issue. Assisted dying is not simply a medical issue concerned with the "suffering body," but it is also a political and legal issue concerning the laws that make such an easing of that suffering possible or impossible based, as this book will argue, on a socio-political logic grounded in the "protection" and "immunization" of life. In short, the problem of assisted dying is a problem of immunization, and the problem of immunization is a problem bound to the very way that immunity causes a closure off—or a "defense" of the borders around the self, as Campbell (2011) puts it. As will become clear throughout the following pages of this book, the problem of assisted dying is intimately linked to the emergence of a rationality of politics that is focused on the closing off and immunization of individual subjects from one another.

This book therefore treats immunization as a political rationality of governance and it treats the law as a particular discourse of this rationality that, at present, brings this rationality into effect. When Campbell refers to immunity as a defense or closure around the subject, he also refers to the exacerbated state of immunity in the context of our contemporary neoliberal forms of governance. These contemporary forms of governance emphasize an ever-increasing division between persons based on social and economic norms of privacy, individual self-interest and a desire not to burden, or be burdened by, others. From this vantage one can note that a concern with immunization is also a concern with the way that immunity mechanisms have the result of drawing us away from relations of a communal nature. In particular, the concern is with how a political emphasis on individual life's protection comes at the expense of the prospect of community (Esposito, 2010, 2011). Communitarians have claimed that under liberal and increasingly neoliberal governance agendas we find ourselves in an increasingly "individualizing society" or a society of "possessive individualism" in which subjects bear less responsibility toward one another and are increasingly self interested (e.g., Friedland and Robertson, 1990; Lasch, 1991; MacPherson, 1962; Olssen, 2010; Peredo, 2011; Putnam, 2000). Neoliberal rationalities of governance lead to a dissociation from values of community (May, 2012; Parkinson and Howarth, 2008), or perhaps better put, they reshape values of community to conform to the rationality itself: a good community or a good subject acting in the name of said community is one in which individuals take care of themselves and do not burden the "whole" (May, 2012; Olssen, 2010).

On the basis of this insight into immunization, this book explores how the fundamental problem of assisted dying can be understood as that which is grounded precisely in the semantics of "assistance" itself: in particular, as this book argues, it is not simply that the law cannot recognize compassionate motives for assisted death; nor is it that the law imposes a problematic paternalism per se. Rather, the fundamental problem is that both the law's inability to recognize compassion and the law's enforcement of paternalism are grounded in a socio-political logic that emphasizes divisive, individualistic conceptions of human behaviors and human relationships: the law does not recognize relationships between subjects that can in any way be deemed "open" to outsiders who might assist with death but instead operates on a series of assumptions (and indeed the law produces these very assumptions) that subjects are closed off from one another and require protection from one another. The problem of assisted dying is attached to a broader problem regarding the limits imposed on acceptable human relations. Decisions on assisted death are implicated in a closing off of subjects, with the effect that, as the New York Task Force on Life and Law (1994) noted, the law "shores up [the] ... limits of human relationships." In the instance of assisted dying the law can only recognize relationships that are divisive and closed.

In short, this book unpacks and explains how a neoliberal emphasis on immunizing relations that are both individualizing and totalizing is problematic because it serves to maintain what de Tocqueville called a society in which subjects "live side by side, unconnected by any common tie:" a society in which we are reciprocally dissociated from one another (Oliva, 2006). The problem of assisted dying is also a problem with a closure off from others, treating subjects as private, personal, proper selves. At base, the problem of assisted dying is attached to a problem of community. This has large implications for those of us interested in assisted death, for what we see in the logic of immunization running through law as a discourse and technology of governance is a drive to protect and immunize each and every individual life from all other communal life outside of it. It is these implications that the present book sets out to explore.

Chapter Outline

In order to explore the implications of immunization for the problem of assisted dying, it is first important to establish more fully the relationship between contemporary forms of governance, the neoliberal nature of law and how the question of assisted dying is attached to a more fundamental question about community. With this in mind the first chapter, Assisted Dying as a Problem of Community, explains how legal decisions on assisted dying reflect a larger system of governance that operates according to an immunizing neoliberal logic that is at once concerned with preserving individual life and at the same time concerned with preserving the notion of communal life. The chapter outlines the way that law operates using "fictions" to establish two poles of an immunity paradigm: the "immune person" and the "immune society" that allow neoliberal immunization to operate as a rationality of governance. This opening chapter establishes the groundwork for the remaining chapters of the book that specifically focus on core concepts emerging from case law that illustrate the particular problem, and illustrate precise ways that law produces an image of this reciprocally dissociated community through the use of different concepts to feed its fictions.

Chapter 2 then begins with an account of the concepts of enmity and vulnerability and their use in the articulation of legal fictions. The chapter concentrates primarily on the example of Nicklinson's legal appeal (England) where these concepts emerged most prominently, and it also draws on other appeals from Taylor (Canada) and Fleming (Ireland) as support for its claims. It reveals how concepts of enmity and vulnerability are used to help the law generate legal fictions of the immune person who is a "proper" subject, and also the legal fiction of the immune society that must protect, but must also be protected from, proper subjects. These two legal fictions assume a necessary confrontation between a vulnerable requestor and the interests of surrounding persons (e.g., family). The decisions of law assume this confrontation in various ways in the different cases, but in each the concept of enmity and its associated vulnerability is used to frame subjects as fixed and knowable: drawing on these concepts allows law to fix as a truth the notion that humanity cannot be trusted and that behavior is universal and predictable. The concepts of enmity and vulnerability are articulated to feed the idea that "man is wolf to man" which in turn feeds the two legal fictions that would rationalize the "protection" and subsequent division and dissociation of subjects from one another sustained through law.

The chapter argues that this use of enmity and vulnerability feeds legal fictions that support competitive, uncompassionate communal relations that frame neoliberal political contexts.

Chapter 3 reveals how, in other cases, law's fictions hold out a view that legal persons—whether vulnerable or not—are entities that cannot be violated in any way. In much the same way as concepts of enmity and vulnerability in Chapter 1, the concept of the inviolable person in Chapter 2 is articulated in order to produce the fiction of law's subjects as divided and individualistic, who are necessarily dissociated and "immunized" from one another. The chapter focuses initially on the case of *Bland*, and also draws on others like *Rodriguez*. It argues that the law makes a distinction between what it calls "acts" of killing (making die) and "omissions" that simply "let die." The former rationalizes what the law calls "passive euthanasia," while allowing law to deny "active" euthanasia and assisted suicide. The law draws on the concept of inviolability to feed a fiction of an immune person whose body is not being interfered with when one simply "pulls the plug" and "lets" a subject die; however, this same concept of inviolability allows the law to deny an act of "killing" or "making" die that would indeed interfere with the fiction of the immune person as a bordered, private subject. This legitimates the death of some "abject" subjects who would otherwise burden the neoliberal immune ethos by seeming to comport with this said ethos.

Chapter 4 argues that in other cases in England and Canada the concept of security feeds the two legal fictions in a dual sense. The chapter argues that the law draws on the concept of security to feed the legal fiction of an "immune society," which is presented as a unified, whole community that is protected from individuals who would threaten this totality. This fiction is generated in order to discount law's other fiction, established in other cases, of the "the immune person," which also relies on the concepts of security and inviolable personhood (discussed in the previous Chapter 3) to underpin it. When these two fictions of the immune society and immune person come into conflict with one another the law will reformulate its fiction of the "immune society" by amending the concept of the "secure person;" it does so by drawing on concepts such as "fundamental justice" and "positive and negative obligations" in support of the immune society as a necessary totality of immune persons. In the same way that law licenses omissions to sustain a fiction of the inviolable person, so too does law license another omission, this time articulated as a "negative obligation" to protect the person: the law folds the concept of the secure person within the legal fiction of the immune society, such that the individual subject of rights is understood as a legal person whose interests are bound to this whole.

Chapter 5 focuses on the way that cases use the concept of dependency to frame subjects who are dependent upon others as degenerate and abject subjects. The chapter argues that the law does not challenge this link between dependency and degeneracy but instead fixes this link through the legal fictions it feeds: while law appears to act benevolently (claiming to deny assisted death in the interests of the "vulnerable"), it does not challenge social norms that construct certain persons as "vulnerable" on the basis of their being dependent and thus the "proper" appellants for assisted death (e.g., elderly, disabled, terminally ill); instead law fixes these subjects as the right kind of subjects for assisted death and therefore as inevitably vulnerable to outside interference. This is a problem because the law does not then challenge the idea that some lives are more worthy than others, but rather it confirms this idea and then claims to protect unworthy life from the interference of outsiders based on its legal fictions. In the process, the fictions reaffirm and shore up images of a private, independent person that founds neoliberal political rationalities.

On the strength of the preceding chapters, the concluding chapter considers an alternative way of approaching assisted death by way of a summary of the concepts and fictions addressed throughout. This affirmative politics focuses on how concepts seem to feed legal fictions around closures and how these closures might be reopened toward an ethos of reciprocity and dependency. Three theses for an affirmative politics of assisted death are outlined: first, law as a practice of critique; second, law as a third person politics; and finally third, law as a open and risky politics.

Notes

1 www.theguardian.com/uk/2012/sep/16/tony-nicklinson-lauren-daughter-euthanasia

2 This differs to active involuntary euthanasia whereby the subject does not consent to death yet the appeal is made on the basis of a "mercy" killing. A key Canadian case of *Latimer* represents this type of euthanasia, whereby a father killed his disabled daughter and appealed his case on the basis of compassion. See *R v Latimer* (2001), 193 D.L.R. (4th) 577 (Sup Ct Can).

Chapter 1

Assisted Dying as a Problem of Community

In much the same way that Durkheim associated the issue of suicide with a shifting social terrain toward dissociative, divisive human relations of anomie and individualism (1979: 8, 11, 288–290, 321), so too can one consider the extent to which assisted dying is also implicated in the relation between the individual and his or her relation to the community. From Durkheim's vantage, excessive individualism as well as insufficient individualism could both lead to a subject enacting suicide: feelings of loneliness may contribute to seeking reprieve in death, as could feelings of excessive obligation and duty to one's community, which could lead to one martyring oneself for the perceived good of the whole. In this regard, the act of suicide cannot simply be understood or examined as a problem of the individual; rather, it must be examined as a potential by-product of a larger sociological issue concerning how individuals relate to another within the larger community.

Indeed, until his insights, scholars had insisted that suicide was a religious or moral question but had not considered that society, and the norms and values that it purports, might shape people's decisions to end their lives. Much the same can be said for discussions of assisted dying: one can and must ask to what extent social norms shape individuals' decisions to appeal for the "right to die" and to what extent social norms also shape the laws that permit some forms of assistance in death (e.g., palliative sedation, passive euthanasia, travelling to Dignitas or another country where assisted death is legal) yet deny other forms (e.g., voluntary active euthanasia, physician-assisted suicide, mercy killing). Appeals to die and laws that deny or permit them do not emerge in a vacuum: they are, as Durkheim noted, reflective of people's perceptions about their relation to themselves and to one another. The person seeking assisted death might claim it is to end their physical suffering but it is also in response to various social perceptions regarding the use and value of the individual within this society and the role they play in relation to others: this is based on the social perception of the "good life." This account of the "good life," as Butler (2012) notes, is a biopolitical and a governmental question. Political rationalities that organize life and "establish a set of measures for the differential valuation of life itself" help to put in place the valuation subjects give to their own lives on the basis of their interaction with and engagement with social determinations of this life: "The most individual question of morality—how do I live this life that is mine?—is bound up with biopolitical questions distilled in forms such these: Whose lives matter? Whose lives do not matter as lives, are not recognizable as living, or count only ambiguously as alive?" (Butler, 2012).[1] The subject of assisted dying is no different.

The Good Life, Immunization and Community

Italian philosopher, Roberto Esposito, notes that modernity's version of the "good life" came to be associated with a life that was deemed to be "protected." This protection took various forms: under Hobbes' conception of sovereign arrangements of power the subject was deemed to be protected from the threat that other individual life posed within a state of nature. Likewise, with the rise of liberalism, protection took on a different meaning: it came to be associated with the notion of individual "rights" to be free and to act in a way that one could have property and ownership over land and one's own body without interference from others. The liberal individual was born and he or she could act independently so long as said individual did not threaten another's shared right to the same independence. Indeed the good life was equivalent with the immunized life—the life that was protected from outside interference and able to live with freedom from others (Esposito, 2011).

Yet this emphasis on life's protection had other implications. In his works *Communitas* (2010) and *Immunitas* (2011), Esposito articulates the rise of immunity alongside the decline of its coterminous concept, community. A concern with individual life's protection emerged, as Esposito notes, at the expense of the prospect of communal forms of life (Esposito, 2010, 2011). Indeed, within Esposito's various works what comes to the fore most prominently is exactly this trade-off between individual life's protection and the protection of forms of community and our exposure toward otherness. We heed a warning within his work of the increasingly privatizing tendencies of modern society that take us away from communal potentials, or the prospects of living together. This is why Esposito's work is particularly insightful for the present book, which is concerned with how the politics of assisted dying is bound to a larger problem regarding the protection of individual life and how this protection of life is implicated in the question of community. Esposito's thesis on a growing "immunization" of society away from communal bonds can therefore help us consider how individualizing techniques that emerge through a neoliberal rationality of governance are attached to larger questions about community and how assisted dying laws and the legal decisions that declare assisted dying to be illegal cannot be thought outside the question of community.

At base, Esposito (2008, 2010, 2011) depicts community as significant, reciprocal obligations imposed on individual members, whose participation in community entails gift giving. In his etymology of community, Esposito (2010) traces community to the root word *munus*, which denotes an obligation to gift-give, fundamental to the heart of community. The *munus* is an expropriative demand; it is a "gift that one gives, but not that one receives" (2010: 5). "It isn't having, but on the contrary is a debt, a pledge, a gift that is to be given and that therefore will establish a lack. The subjects of a community are united by an obligation, in the sense that we say 'I owe you something', but not 'you owe me something'" (Esposito 2010: 6).[2] As an expropriative demand, the gift is a type of duty in Esposito's terminology (2010: 4–5). It is a "gift that one must give and because one cannot not give ... It doesn't by any means imply the stability of a possession and even less the acquisition of something dynamic and earned, but loss, subtraction, transfer" (2010: 5). "What predominates in the munus is, in other words, reciprocity or 'mutuality' of giving that assigns the one to the other in an obligation" (2010: 5). What unites us in this obligation is not some "thing," or "property." Relations are not constituted through something additive that is shared such as blood, birth or common identity but "a lack, a limit that is configured as onus" (Esposito, 2010: 6).

This notion of community is historical: *communitas,* in all neo-Latin languages has referred to "what is not proper;" what is common "begins where the proper ends" (2010: 3). Humans have always lived in common. It is a fundamental aspect of humankind to be in common; to have an obligation to one another. Indeed, "We need community because it is the very locus or, better, the transcendental condition of our existence, given that we have always existed in common," notes Esposito (2012c: 14). Esposito thus reveals a "law of community"

(2012c: 14) that he says sustains the appearance of what is held in common as a distinct entity (that is, as a proper community) by placing unyielding demands on individuals to give themselves and their support to others. The law of community is thus "the exigency according to which we feel obligated not to lose this originary condition" (2012c: 14). For him, being in community is necessary; nothing is more important or necessary than this question of community. Given its underscoring "donative obligation" and a "law of care" toward others, community has an affirmative meaning (Esposito 2012c: 59).

While communal being is necessary, Esposito also speaks of its paradox. Community can never be fully realized because it is founded on a debt or a lack. It is founded on the demands that it places on individuals and because of this community always threatens to undermine the agent who is giving. "We inhabit the margin between what we owe and what we can do," says Esposito (2012c: 15), because to fulfill the possibility of community it will always undermine the one from which it is constituted. Community will always undermine the possibility of the individual subject. It is for this reason that community "presents us with an enigma: impossible and necessary" (2012c: 26).

Community, thus, does not exist per se; that is to say that community is not some "thing" but rather is "the 'relation'—the 'with' or the 'between'—that joins multiple subjects" (2012c: 29). It is not an "entity" but rather is a "non-entity" "... that precedes and cuts every subject, wresting him or her from identification with himself or herself and submitting him or her to irreducible alterity" (2012c: 29). Because community is not something that can be forged through the unity of individuals, but rather demands that the unit of the individual itself is opened out to heterogeneity rather than identification, demands for community or from the community are always demands that individuals cannot fully respond to, for if they do they risk themselves, which in turn risks the very subjects from which the possibility of community derives. The communal lack, or a negatively defined community, is thus articulated as a danger to the possibility of individual identity. The dependence of the *munus* on the subject, and the subject's obligation to community, forever threatens the possibility of a "self" or identity. Campbell neatly states this point. He writes:

> this debt or obligation of gift giving operates as a kind of originary defect for those belonging to a community. The defect revolves around the pernicious effects of reciprocal donation on individual identity. Accepting the munus directly undermines the capacity of

> the individual to identify himself or herself as such and not as part of the community.
>
> (Campbell, 2008: x)

The mechanism of protection of the individual from this donative obligation is what I have already described via a brief discussion of law as community's opposite form, immunity. Immunity is a concept that occupies a place across the biological and medical sciences, as well as the political sciences, referring in the former to a defense against disease and infection or biological invasion, and in the latter to a political exemption or a form of safe passage—a protection from prosecution (Esposito, 2008, 2010). Like *communitas*, *immunitas* derives from the *munus*, meaning gift, duty, obligation, but where *communitas* is affirmative, "immunitas is negative" (Esposito, 2012c: 59). Immunity emerges given the threat of community to individual identity and thus *immunitas* operates alongside community by granting a *dispensatio* from this obligation to gift give. *Immunitas*, therefore, takes on a negative meaning in which, through immunization, one no longer owes a debt to the community in the form of gift giving, and instead merely becomes a beneficiary. Immunization is thus articulated as a protective endeavor, or as a mechanism that blocks the threat of the excessive demands of the *munus*.[3] As Esposito, notes, immune is "he or she who has no obligations towards the other and can therefore conserve his or her own essence in tact as a subject and owner of himself or herself" (2012c: 39). Immunity is appropriative rather than expropriative, and allows us to forge instances of the "proper," noted earlier.

According to Esposito, mechanisms of immunization have historically generated various prosthetic kinds of institutional or discursive political mechanisms that are said to protect life from its own excesses by forging proper ways of being. Law is one such instance of immunization and is arguably the most central and originary immunity apparatus. Modes of immunization are therefore political practices that are ultimately norms over life that designate ways of living in order to prevent risks to this life. Immunization is therefore a matter of individual security and with this individual security comes a crisis of community.

Neoliberalism and a Crisis of Community

Esposito's concern with the relation between immunization and community is also shared by a number of other scholars who reflect on the increasingly privatizing tendencies of modern society that take us away from communal potentials, or the prospects of living together. A large body of work claims that the contemporary political rationality is neoliberal (e.g., Beeson and Firth, 1998; Campbell, 2011; Foucault, 2008; Lemke, 2002; Rose, 1993, 1999), which, with its increasing emphasis on privatization and individualization, leads to a decline in communal bonds and forms of living. As noted in the introduction, communitarians have claimed that we are in an increasingly individualizing society whereby subjects bear less responsibility toward one another (e.g., Friedland and Robertson, 1990; Lasch, 1991; MacPherson, 1962; Olssen, 2010; Peredo, 2011; Putnam, 2000). Neoliberal rationalities of governance thus re-articulate community values in accordance with this rationality, meaning that individuals are encouraged to demonstrate responsibility for themselves and are also encouraged not to burden the society as a "whole" (May, 2012; Olssen, 2010). Indeed, as Esposito notes in our contemporary neoliberal era we have witnessed a "substantial growth in immunization" (2012c: 130). Such neoliberal governance agendas and dispositifs reorient social relations around enterprise and are highly contentious. As McNay (2009: 64) writes, "The orchestration of individual existence as enterprise atomizes our understanding of social relations, eroding collective values and intersubjective bonds of duty and care at all levels of society."

As a particular mechanism of governmentality, neoliberalism structures possible fields of action in particular ways. This also means that neoliberal political rationalities generate neoliberal subjects (Brown, 2005; Cruikshank, 1999; Rose, 1993) and these subjects discipline themselves according to the political rationality that demands subjects treat themselves as business entities: in this regard, social relationships are "defined in terms of market alliances" (Gershon and Alexy, 2011: 801). To generate this neoliberal subject, political rationalities of governance generate and inculcate values of self-interest, and establish the conditions such that self-interest can be pursued (Foucault, 2008). This requires that neoliberal rationalities encourage "disconnection," which is something "people labour to achieve" (Gershon and Alexy, 2011: 802). This means to suggest that neoliberal immunization is not a natural condition but rather it is a symptom of this particular neoliberal rationality of governance (Foucault, 2008; Lemke, 2002; Rose, 1999). Where a neoliberal immune rationality is oriented toward individualism, such displays of dissociated and self-interested human behavior and such a shift from communal values—or, perhaps better put, a shift toward different ideas of what constitutes communal values—are simply behaviors that are perpetuated through discourses that instill and inculcate "a particular anthropology of man" (Read, 2009); that is to say that the way we relate to one another is shaped by discourses, enunciated through mechanisms of governance, that construct certain truths about human nature and human behavior in order to codify how we relate to one another in line with the rationality of governance.

One of the particulars of a neoliberal rationality is the ways in which it shapes conduct by articulating persons as economic subjects, *homo economicus*. A neoliberal rationality of governance shapes its subjects as "entrepreneurs" of themselves and encourages—indeed makes possible—this entrepreneurship of the self by engendering fields of action that incite the pursuit of individual interests (Foucault, 2009: 228). This view of a neoliberal political rationality as a governmentality that structures fields of action is different to the classic liberal idea of governance: where the latter believed that a self-regulating economy would curb state interference, the former operates according to a governance agenda that interferes with society and sets the very conditions for the possibility of a seemingly self-regulating market place to emerge (Foucault, 2008). It does so by forging the social, economic and political conditions to support the possibility of the emergence and intensification of economic subjects (Foucault, 2008).

As such, a subject's value is based on his or her ability to function as an individual as part of a larger whole (Brown, 2005); a neoliberal political rationality values subjects if they are increasingly entrepreneurial, self-sufficient and can take care of themselves economically, and if they do not burden the state or other private economic subjects (Brown, 2005). As per Brown's (2005) commentary, a neoliberal subject strategically situates himself or herself as an individual entrepreneur who is increasingly divorced from public concerns in favor of private interest. The shift away from a social welfare model toward new political emphases on privatization and individual responsibility (Wacquant, 2010) forges new neoliberal subjectivities whereby persons' worth and their internalization of this worth is measured according to how well they can function as independent economic subjects within the larger totality of the state (Brown, 2005; Mihic, 2008). This is not a "natural" condition (as some classic economic theorists had claimed), but is instead a manufactured condition shaped by rationalities of governance (Foucault, 2008).

Campbell (2011) brings the discussion of neoliberalism directly into conversation with the prospect of community. From Campbell's vantage, a pastoral logic of power in neoliberalism has not dissipated but rather has intensified by increasingly emphasizing individualization within the larger totality. According to Campbell (2011), a neoliberal governmentality structures fields of conduct in ways that increasingly divide subjects from communal relations; neoliberalism is problematic because it emphasizes and inculcates technologies that sustain the protection of individual interests and a symbiotic dissociation from communal interests, and in turn is tied to the manifestation and erection of "a defense of the self and its borders" (Campbell, 2011: 119). More specifically, drawing on Esposito's insights, Campbell (2010, 2011) argues that a neoliberal governmentality establishes human relations in increasingly "immunized" ways.

Specific to neoliberal immunization is an ethos that is divisive yet also totalizing. The individualizing, dissociative ethos of neoliberalism that divides individuals from one another is also part of a totalizing ethos that claims to unite these dissociative individuals through a shared goal of "reciprocal dissociation:" what neoliberal immunized individuals share is their common dissociation from positive obligations and duties toward one another in favor of minimal interference not only from the state but also from other individual neoliberal subjects. From Esposito's vantage, where immunity mechanisms have been inscribed over time, today we live in a society that aims for the common division of persons from one another: "... society is legally governed and unified by the principle of common separation: the only thing in common is in the claim to whatever is individual, just as the object of public law is precisely the safeguarding of that which is private" (Esposito, 2011: 25).

Only a few commentators have situated assisted dying in this contemporary governmental context. Writing with reference to the 1975 Quinlan case and 1990 Cruzan case, Pelaprat and Hartouni (2012: 199) note the "new kind of social, legal, economic and ethical actor" arose in the neoliberal era. They argue that the right to die emerged as part of a "neoliberal ontology" of freedom based on personal choice, personal interest and autonomy. In their opinion "right to die" legal appeals provided evidence that a new subject of power had emerged who would exercise freedom in a way that was consistent with neoliberal individualism. Pelaprat and Hartouni (2012) identify that appellants of assisted dying conform to neoliberal subjectivities. Mihic (2008) also writes on assisted dying in the contemporary political context. She also suggests that subjective right to die appeals are not "freely" made by liberal individuals; rather, the right to die appeal might be construed as the exertion of a freedom that is shaped by the social context in which the "choice" emerges. One cannot simply claim that a liberal individual's appeal to the "right to die" is entirely "free" without also considering how this liberal individual's "freedom" is constituted within a broader governance agenda (Mihic, 2008; Tierney, 2006). In this regard one must consider the prospect that freedom is not the opposite of governance but, on the contrary, is a mechanism of governance (Rose, 1999). Mihic (2008) proposes that assisted dying emerges as a problem because subjects internalize a neoliberal ethos. Neoliberalism creates subjects who believe themselves to be free and "unfettered by the state;" however, by contrast, "this putatively free juridical subject is not autonomous as claimed but reconstituted to fit the socio-economic order in the form of human capital" (Mihic, 2008: 167). With reference to assisted dying, she continues: "advocates of physician assisted suicide conceive of the self as human capital" (Mihic, 2008: 170). The neoliberal subject is one whose value is measured as human capital on the basis of investment and productivity (Campbell, 2011: 73). From Mihic's (2008: 180) vantage, interpreting the right to die via human capital means that we must consider how:

> the supposedly autonomous dying patient is supposed to take into consideration the welfare of her or his loved ones. On the neoliberal human capital model, parents who love their children will try to close the self like a firm; they will try to die as efficiently as possible.

Mihic's neoliberal subject has a different drive than that which Pelaprat and Hartouni (2012) suggested. Where the latter argued that the neoliberal assisted dying ethos is one concerned only with one's self (i.e. one seeks to die because one considers it a way of asserting one's autonomy), Mihic seems to think there is a communal or social aspect to the problem. She suggests for example that not only is neoliberalism concerned that subjects internalize the belief that they are acting autonomously and independently, but also neoliberalism is concerned that subjects respect the autonomy and independence of others. The problem of assisted dying is thus implicated not only in an individualizing mode of governance (concerning one's own autonomy/self) but also in a totalizing mode of governance (respecting and ensuring the autonomy and the self of everyone else). Appellants of assisted dying might be concerned with how their existence as a subject who can no longer act autonomously without assistance presents them as a burden and as an interference with the freedom of other neoliberal agents (i.e.

trapped in their bodies and dependent on others, as Rodriguez and Nicklinson noted).

In short, where Pelaprat and Hartouni (2012) identify the individualizing aspect of the politics of assisted dying within a neoliberal political rationality, Mihic (2008) identifies the other important social and communal element: it is not simply that subjects become more individualized within neoliberalism and that the exercise of subjective "rights to die" are neoliberal in that they are simply reflective of the individualizing pole of a neoliberal rationality of governance; rather, this individualization of subjects also has a communal element and has a social effect regarding the way we relate to one another within the larger community and totality of persons. Assisted dying appeals might emerge not only because one is concerned with one's own privacy and individuality, but also because one does not want to impose oneself onto others: individualization has a communal element in the sense that we are "reciprocally" disconnected from one another under this totalizing logic. A good neoliberal subject is not simply self-interested but rather is socially interested in preserving the self-interest of other individual actors. Though neoliberalism might operate on the basis of individualization, its pastoral roots ensure that its logic is also totalizing and that neoliberal subjects operate as part of this totality and with this totality in mind (e.g., Esposito, 2008, 2010; Foucault, 2009; Oliva, 2006). This is an aspect of neoliberal rationality that other scholars have commented on more broadly, not in relation to assisted dying, but with reference to the politics of community.

Law and Neoliberal Immunization

Conceiving of neoliberalism as a political rationality is different to conceiving of it simply as an economic theory or as an ideology: the former vantage emphasizes how neoliberalism is a strategy of governance (Rose, 1993). This means to suggest that neoliberalism is a form of "governmentality," which frames subjects' conduct (Hamman, 2009). Rose prefers to call this governmental account "advanced liberalism" as opposed to "neoliberalism," possibly to differentiate between these two ideas of governance (Rose, 1993, 2000).[4] Neoliberalism or advanced liberalism as a governmentality takes its cue from the Foucaultian insight that claims the types of rule we are subjected to are not absolute sources of power (Rose, 1993, 1999). Advanced liberal rule is dependent upon different governance strategies or techniques than neoliberal ideological rule; it uses experts in different ways. "It does not seek to govern through 'society' but through the regulated choices of individual citizens" (Rose, 1993: 285). It also seeks to "detach substantive authority of expertise from the apparatuses of political rule, relocating experts within a market governed by the rationalities of competition, accountability and consumer demand" (Rose, 1993: 285).

Law plays a role in constituting this condition, and is also constituted by it (Golder and Fitzpatrick, 2009) and the experts called into cases, in addition to the judges making the final decision on cases and the appellants themselves are all subjects bound within this governance strategy. "Neo-liberalism is a constructivist project," states Brown (2003), "... it does not presume the ontological givenness of a thoroughgoing economic rationality for all domains of society, but rather takes as its task the development, dissemination and institutionalization of such a rationality."[5] As a conduit for such dissemination and institutionalization, law plays a vital role (Golder, 2011). Neoliberal rationalities of governance purport certain conditions as natural or necessary, despite these conditions being entirely constructed; from the vantage of law, all legal decisions are constructed despite their presentation as truth. Law operates as a discourse to normalize the rationality of governance that aims to present such disconnection between subjects as "an entropic and inevitable end" rather than something that is inculcated into people's subjectivities as that which they "labour to achieve" to become good neoliberal citizens, as Gershon and Alexy note (2011: 802). The law becomes a regulatory apparatus or technology of this neoliberal political rationality. In doing so, the law acts as a norm (Rose and Valverde, 1998).

While legal analysis may be problematic when law is regarded as an independent governing body, a neutral or autonomous practice, or a handmaiden of the state, legal analysis is highly fruitful and necessary when law is understood as a discourse that is both shaped by the context in which it finds itself and is also constituting of this very context (Golder and Fitzpatrick, 2009; Rose and Valverde, 1998; Smith, 2000; Valverde, 2003). This is to suggest, as Pavlich (2012a: 1) has done, that law and legal judgments do not arise in isolation but must be understood as a "shifting product of local and wider power-knowledge formations;" from this vantage the law is deployed discursively and tactically as a site of "governmental dispersal" (Golder and Fitzpatrick, 2009: 33). Golder and Fitzpatrick, for instance, refer to Foucault (1990a: 36) who had expressed quite clearly that in contemporary society "the law operates more as a norm." In presenting itself as a truth, and operating as a norm, law must operate discursively. For its part, the law operating as a discourse is a technology of governance that plays a role in constituting the political rationality of governance and thus is implicated in shaping these human behaviours and relations that are associated with it (and necessary to sustain it) (Golder and Fitzpatrick, 2009).[6]

In the same way that one cannot separate the medical issue of assisted dying from the legal terrain that governs the prospects of this practice, Amy Swiffen (2011) also reminds us that one cannot separate bioethical matters such as the question of assisted dying from questions of jurisprudence. Ethical arguments based on questions concerning the values of life and the prospect of death are always implicated in matters of legal decision-making that are also, always, implicated in larger socio-political discussions. The law permits or denies forms of assisted death on the basis that law has some "stake" in the decision. There is a reason—or perhaps multiple reasons—why the law is invested in its decision. Indeed, this investment of law in decisions over matters of the "good life" is perhaps why Adalgiso Amendola (2012) has referred to contemporary bioethical dilemmas that occupy places within legal discussion as "bio-juridical" ones. Moreover, if law has a stake in determining the "good life," it is also constitutive and constituting of broader governance agendas that shape what this good life looks like (Golder and Fitzpatrick, 2009).

Echoing these sentiments, and refusing the expulsion thesis as well as rejecting literature that examines the scientificity of law and legal reasoning (e.g., Brewer, 1998), one cannot reveal the principles of law per se but rather one can focus on the "the deployment of knowledges within and in relation to law, wherever that occurs, prioritizing questions of epistemological authority and sidelining doctrinal questions" (Valverde, 2003: 21). With this view of law as a backdrop one can reconceptualize the problem of assisted dying, focusing instead on law as a site of analysis that is enframed within a broader logic of governance. Valverde's work suggests something similar is possible. She argues that case law is an excellent site through which to analyze this possibility. Where case law is part of the common law legal system, also known as "judge made law," case law is also based on judges' interpretation of statutes that have emerged in previous cases known as precedents. Precedents are legally binding, and the more they are affirmed in law, the more they become entrenched. Case law also draws on opinions, beliefs and research from "experts" such as medical practitioners, lawyers, academics, politicians and others who have contributed to a body of knowledge, presenting a number of different viewpoints on the subject area (Smith, 2000; Valverde, 2003).[7] As such, case law is an overt site in which one can examine knowledge constitution. As she suggests, "the parties to a legal case can be said to constitute knowledge in the very process of using it, while courts and tribunals can be usefully regarded as further constituting knowledge in the process of examining evidence and drawing conclusions from it" (Valverde, 2003: 5).

From these vantages, law (e.g., Golder and Fitzpatrick, 2009; Iveson, 1998; Pavlich, 2012a, 2012b; Rose and Valverde, 1998), and more specifically case law (e.g., Smith, 2000; Valverde, 2003), is not a site of truth, but instead is a site of constitutive knowledge; one ought not simply to take for granted the *ratio decidendi*—or the reason of the decision at face value—and instead ought to consider law as a discourse (Tadros, 1998). To consider law as such means to consider how law is comprised of different constructed concepts that legitimate law as an authority of truth (Pavlich, 2012a, 2012b). The constructed concepts are historically specific because law operating as a discourse emerges in a particular context that shapes what discourses become more dominant than others. Because legal discourses are enunciative of a broader political rationality of governance they are also understood as "governmental technologies," which means they bring into effect the political rationality. When law and its subjects are viewed through this lens, one must move away from accounts of law that emphasize individual subjects' "rights" appeals as those which fight against a state enforced law and instead one must consider the nuances of how subjects and the law itself are discursively constructed. Based on this argument, one must also then find ways to move beyond the arguments of those who could be described as "classic liberals" who stipulate that individual "rights to die" must be met with legal progressivism.

One of the most well known public scholarly discussions on assisted dying that emphasized this matter of liberal rights to die was articulated in the *Philosopher's Brief*, published in 1997 by six renowned liberal philosophers including Ronald Dworkin, Thomas Nagel, Robert Nozik, John Rawls, Thomas Scanlon and Judith Jarvis Thompson. They submitted as *amici curiae* information to the Supreme Court in support of the respondents in the United States' legal case of *Washington v Glucksburg* [1997] regarding the legality of assisted suicide. Their brief brought together numerous arguments in favor of voluntary active euthanasia. Citing the 1992 case of *Planned Parenthood v Casey*, 505 U.S. 833, 851, for example, they noted that "... It flows from the right of people to make their own decisions about matters 'involving the most intimate and personal choices a person may make in a lifetime, choices central to personal dignity and autonomy'" (1997: 434). Furthermore, individual subjects, they argued, have the right to a "personal decision such as the timing and moment of one's death" (1997: 434).

At base, their discussion framed the question of assisted dying by way of a power struggle between a liberal desire for the freedom and autonomy of individuals versus the paternalistic, indeed odious, tyranny of the state (Dworkin, 1993). Such a liberal perspective also enters into the dialogue in legal cases on assisted dying themselves: liberal scholarly work that advocates assisted dying is often cited as "evidence" or "expertise" in legal cases (e.g., Dworkin is cited in *Rodriguez v British Columbia*). Problematically, however, these arguments are bound within a framework that does not consider how law gets used and adopted from a governmental vantage. In this regard individuals are said to exercise their rights freely and in opposition to the law which is viewed simply as "paternal" and as that which imposes a blanket ban on assisted death that contradicts individuals rights not to be interfered with by state systems of governance. Indeed these arguments suggest that the law's duty as a democratic law of the people is to respect these fundamental rights to rational self-direction.[8]

In much the same vein, one must also move beyond the views of those who defend law's denial of assisted death in order to allegedly protect claims to "vulnerable" life (e.g., Davis, 2004; Smith, 2006). This position that espouses the need to protect life claims that vulnerable subjects, particularly those who experience disability, are elderly, or terminally ill, require protection from persons who might want to harm them. Those who occupy this position typically base their arguments on the prospect that appellants might be coerced into desiring their own death. Their arguments are also based on alleged fears that other persons who have yet to appeal to the right to die but are depicted as members of vulnerable populations might, were the practice of assisted dying legalized, feel compelled to die based on a "duty" conferred upon them (e.g. Cholbi, 2010; Davis, 2004; Hardwig, 1997; Smith, 2006). This duty to die is not articulated as a covertly imposed duty; rather, it is a duty that some public voices have overtly articulated. Academics such as Kissel (2000), for instance, argue quite visibly that a duty to die ought to be inculcated from an early age. She suggests that individuals should be encouraged to sacrifice themselves if they are to otherwise burden their family. She also argues that children should learn the economic and social benefits of family member's deaths if these family members might burden the family, such as a sibling experiencing a disability who should be removed from life support given the associated medical and legal bills.[9] This type of rhetoric concerning disability and the social and economic burden associated with it bears remnants from remarks of social eugenicists such as Herbert Spencer whose thoughts emerged prominently within the mid 19th century (Turner and Stagg, 2006). Baroness Mary Warnock, who is a member of the UK House of Lords and a strong advocate of euthanasia, also voiced the opinion that elderly persons and those that are ill and that burden their families ought to "creep off and get out of the way." In an interview with the *London Times* she famously equated practices of euthanasia with sacrifice, noting: "in other contexts, sacrificing oneself for one's family would be considered good. I don't see what is so horrible about the motive of not wanting to be an increasing nuisance."[10] This commentary has sparked much debate from those who instead claim that that these arguments in favor of a duty to die seem to be closely associated with the eugenics programs brought into effect through, and culminating with, the atrocities of Nazi Germany (e.g., Davis, 2004; Smith, 2006).

Rather than considering liberal rights appeals to be emergent from independent, individual subjects who are divorced from the state, or taking a view that subjects require blanket legal protection from persons in the community who would otherwise compel such persons to die, a socio-political analysis provides an opportunity to consider how legal rights appeals and the laws they appeal against are bound to the larger social, historical, economic and political context in which they emerge. Indeed, when law and legal decisions are understood as discourses that reflect a larger rationality of governance one can begin to see how law reflects and produces decisions in line with this logic. This is to say that law and legal decisions are able to help realize and sustain a political reality by producing various fictions about human nature that help support the political ethos. Law does this by constructing concepts, or drawing on previously constructed concepts, in order to generate these "legal fictions." These fictions appear as truths via the discourse of law. Judgments of law appear as judgments of "truth," despite these judgments being discursively constructed according to the particular political rationality of the time. In short, law is comprised of various concepts that generate narratives that the feed legal fictions, which express a truth of some kind or are understood as ready-made syntheses. Law is a site in which various concepts, beliefs, notions and knowledges are invented, amended or disregarded. Law is not a passive practice but rather continues to redefine itself and redefine the social context in and through which it emerges (Golder and Fitzpatrick, 2009; Smith, 2000).

Giles Deleuze and Felix Guattari (1991) argued that philosophy is the creation of concepts. Jurisprudence, or the philosophy of law, is also the creation of concepts. Concepts are abstract ideas and imaginary constructions. To focus on wording and concepts in legal cases is to focus on imaginary constructions. If concepts are imaginary and yet they also underpin legal judgments then they are, as some scholars have called them, "fictive" (Picciotto, 1999): the narratives that law produces through its uptake or production of concepts (or its extension of concepts to areas in which the concept has yet to be applied) is a "legal fiction." As such, a neoliberal political rationality is perpetuated and encompassed in concepts that emerge as the building blocks of law and law's fictions. Examining the wording of cases allows one to address what concepts emerge within the wording of cases and how these concepts are the building blocks of particular kinds of narratives that frame specific judgments.

Law's Neoliberal Fictions

According to Henry Maine (1861) the concept of the legal fiction derives from the Roman "fictiones." In old Roman law, "fictio" referred to a term of pleading (Knauer, 2010; Maine, 1861). It was a false allegation or statement that the law would not allow the defendant to contest. Fuller (1967: 9) defines a legal fiction as "... either (1) a statement propounded with a complete or partial consciousness of its falsity, or (2) a false statement recognised as having utility." Olivier (1975: 48) similarly calls a legal fiction "the technical artifice of thought by which an *assumptio contra veritatem* is made." Advocates of legal fictions argue that they are necessary to correct injustices. William Blackstone (Morrison, 2013) had commented on such importance of legal fictions. He argued that even though fictions may "startle" students of law, one must note their necessity. Indeed in the defense of legal fictions he asserted the legal maxim "*in fictione juris semper subsistit aequitas*" (all legal fictions are founded in equity). From his vantage a legal fiction serves as a correction of an injustice or it fills a potential lacuna in law; it is therefore an equitable feature of modern law.

Fuller (1967), by contrast, noted that legal fictions not only produce injustices because of their production and perpetuation of untruths, but also that legal fictions serve as an ideological structure to enable a rationalization of law maker's decisions (Lanza-Kaduce and Bishop, 1986). This is an absolutely key point: legal fictions produce a sense of reality that permits decisions to pass as truths. As Picciotto (1999: 3) notes, the legal fiction emerges through laws and regulations that are "defined by abstract, and hence fictitious, categories." While there are many different approaches to the concept of the legal fiction, in common is the belief that the fiction allows law to operate in a normalizing and regulatory way. There is a prescriptive aspect of fictions, as Bentham noted: the regulatory power of fictions could encourage people to conform to norms.

Within a neoliberal rationality, legal fictions do not just render concepts shifting or tentative, but rather they tend to fix these shifting or tentative concepts in particular ways in accordance with the political rationality. There is a fixed or predictable pattern to the neoliberal legal fictions, of which the concepts that frame and feed such fictions sustain. As Foucault had noted (1990a), law constitutes knowledges as truths, which are enunciative of broader historically specific power-knowledge regimes. It is not that the juridical fiction reveals a deeper truth that is being concealed; rather it is that the juridical fiction reveals the fictive nature of law itself: it reveals all law as jurisprudence. Simply put, law is grounded in concepts that are "made up." Fictions sustain fictions. Legal fictions not only create and feed a narrative that supports a judicial decision, but they also shape a fictive image of a broader mechanism of politics of which this judicial decision is a part (Pavlich, 2013).

Esposito (2012a, 2012b, 2013) does not use the language of legal fiction in his work, but he does point to the fictive base and the regulatory and normalizing power of particular legal concepts. His work on immunization reveals how concepts emerge in ways that create divisive fictions that are part of a broader operation of power-knowledge (what he calls immunization, or what Foucault calls governmentality—both of which are concerned with the relation between the individual and society/community). Mechanisms of immunization emerge to articulate and reinforce concepts that feed legal fictions at the core of a neoliberal ethos. They are, at base, operative in the generation of legal fictions in a neoliberal era.

Immunization is a helpful theoretical construct to draw on in addition to Foucault's thesis on governmentality to think about the operation of legal fictions in assisted dying law. In particular it is useful because it enables us to focus on how legal concepts feed legal fictions that share in common the erection of defensive borders around the self and other. Esposito's analysis on immunization prioritizes this as a central feature of modern systems of governance. Considering the mechanism of immunization then allows one to more precisely locate the concepts in legal cases that generate fictions and feed a neoliberal ethos that share in common divisive and individualizing strategies. It also allows us to consider the process by which law is able to identify its precise object of governance by articulating its object as what Esposito calls "proper." To be proper is to give the form of a totality, or an absolute unity; to be proper is to be a fixed subject under law. From Esposito's vantage nothing is ever absolutely proper; it is a fiction of immunization mechanisms in neoliberal politics. For us, the law, which is a technology of governance, articulates its fictions in accordance with this idea of the proper in order to establish its fictions as truths.

Earlier I noted a concern regarding the link between the problem with assisted dying laws and the prospect of community. Esposito shares a similar concern, albeit a broader one regarding the relation between individuals and others and how immunization mechanisms shore up the limits of these relations via the constitution of the proper. Here we are similarly concerned with how concepts emerging as legal fictions shore up limits of our relationships that precludes the possibility of assistance in death unless this assistance is articulated in ways that are complicit with the neoliberal ethos of division and individuality. Esposito's work is also useful because it sets itself apart from other work exploring legal fictions on the specific topic of personhood. Where the majority of scholarship speaks to the fictive nature of corporate personhood, for example, Esposito also comments on the fictive nature of personhood as a broader concept. He argues that the concept of the "person" has, historically, been constituted as a legal concept in order to allow some "types" of humans to be included in law and protected, and to permit others to be excluded from law. Fagundes (2001) has noted a similar use of the concept of the person that he describes sometimes as a legal fiction and sometimes as a legal metaphor, but both times with attention to the social emphasis on the meaning of the uptake of personhood: this is what he calls the "expressive" dimension of law. Law's uptake of personhood reveals not only law's reflection of social ideals that get incorporated into the use of concepts that feed narratives and fictions, but it also reveals how law shapes these social ideals through the generation of these fictions. As Bentham had also noted, legal fictions are constitutive of norms and are also constituting of them.

For Esposito, the concept of personhood, like the concept of sexuality from Foucault's vantage, is a tactically constituted and constituting concept (it is produced but it also produces) that feeds narratives and ideas about human behavior and human nature—it shapes and defines "who" one "is." It also feeds narratives about who one can become, and how one can be. This feature of allowing law to define its object and rule in ways that conform to a political rationality also allows the law to operate according to other divisive mechanisms. Socio-legal scholars such as Lacey (2001a, 2001b, 2007), Naffine (2003) and Pavlich (2007, 2012a, 2012b, 2013) have also recognized the importance of paying attention to the articulation of the concepts of persons and personhood within law. They have noted that legal processes play an important role in ordering the social realm, allowing law to fix its gaze on a particular subject who becomes the very object of law and the legal judgment (e.g. Pavlich, 2013). How law fixes its gaze has much to do with the political rationalities enunciated within the context in which legal judgments are given (Pavlich, 2013), and cannot be understood apart from a wider contextualization of socio-political, economic and historical factors influencing and intersecting with law (Lacey, 2007).

In the current social climate, the use of legal rights and personhood effectuated through law (such as the corporate person, human rights and so on) that allege to protect subjects are also dividing mechanisms. They are dividing in the sense of who can access legal protection, and they are also dividing in the sense that they constitute the notion of who belongs to the proper community and how one must perform as a proper subject if one wants to belong to this community. In order to belong to the proper political community, one must perform as both as subject who can access rights, which means that one must perform as an individual bounded subject. The neoliberal subject of rights is the subject who belongs to an "immune community" or proper community that is held in common by its reversal of *communitas*: it is held in common by a reciprocal *non-obligation* and reciprocal independence and immunization. For Campbell (2011) one can find a heightened instance of this immunized community in our current "neoliberal era" which is understood as an increasingly privatizing, individualizing and dividing political rationality. What holds us in common in this community is not an obligation toward one another that is expropriative (i.e. that asks us to give to others and obligate ourselves to them) but rather one that is continually appropriative, whereby we are bound by an imperative to be private individuals and to not interfere with or to obligate one another.

In short, if legal fictions are enunciations of discourses of law that generate specific judgments that reinforce the wider neoliberal political rationality then legal decisions and judgments are not truths per se but are constructed through a variety of concepts and fictions that reflect a prevailing governance ethos. To understand law as a discourse that operates more as a norm means to understand law to be comprised of various concepts that generate certain fictions, which sustain truths about how law governs. These narratives sustain law as a ready-made synthesis: law operates discursively; legal judgments draw on and create legal fictions as justifications that in turn feed a broader rationality of governance, the governmentality, that seeks to rule in particular ways. As a site of knowledge constitution, case law produces "legal fictions." Because different parties are involved in constituting knowledge, and because these knowledges are shaped by and shaping of the broader political rationality of governance, reasons outlined in case law for its denial of assisted dying cannot simply be taken as truth since law is neither objective nor neutral; rather, law's reasoning is discursive, meaning that what it presents as truths or facts are contextually established "ways of knowing," or "juridical fictions" constituted within specific "regimes of knowledge" (Foucault, 1981, 1991b, 1991c).

The Immune Person and the Immune Society

Campbell claims that neoliberal's immunizing protection of life is drifting toward what he calls the "thanatopolitical" tendencies of Nazism, the difference between the two becoming "smaller and smaller" (Campbell, 2011: 72). Indeed as Esposito notes, one of the problems with the immunization of life is precisely the problem that Pavlich (2002) has also mentioned: when law imposes protection over life according to certain kinds of proper truths, it closes life off to other possibilities and ways of being. For Esposito this closure of life is not simply one that confines life to particular norms; it also always risks the prospect of life itself. For this book the closure of life is found in the ways that the discourse of law reflects and reconstitutes neoliberal rationalities of governance that divide subjects from one another, and the ways that subjects come to internalize these norms, also dividing themselves from one another.

Rosella Bonito Oliva (2006) argues that in our current political moment with the heightened immunization we are living in an "immune community." She describes the emergence of an inverse of community's originary framework of a positive obligation toward one another. For her, the contemporary present moment is reflective of a slow immunizing transition arising through law. In seeking to protect life from the larger community, law founds itself as an immunity mechanism that shelters life from excessive communal demands. In doing so law formulates and constitutes a new community that Esposito (2010,

2013) calls a "proper community." The proper community emerges as each individual receives a dispensation from the obligations toward one another. The proper community in the contemporary neoliberal arrangement is articulated as a community of divided, independent individuals. Esposito (2010, 2012a, 2013) notes that while immunity was once conceived of as a privilege, in our contemporary society immunity is now instead something seemingly conferred upon all subjects. This is precisely why Campbell (2011) has claimed that in the contemporary climate in which we find ourselves, we have reached a zenith of immunization; we are all immunized from one another; we are in an absolute expression of an immune community (Oliva, 2006).

The concept of the immune community is a useful heuristic device: it emphasizes the pastoral roots of governance that is grounded in the relation between the individual and community (Foucault, 2009); it demands that an analysis pays attention to how the request and denial of assisted dying seems to replicate an immunization of the self from others. Esposito's insight helps one explain how law creates concepts to rationalize its judgments and how these rationalized judgments are part of a larger neoliberal political rationality that seeks to divide, or immunize, subjects from one another. To bring this immune community into being, judicial decisions on assisted dying create two key legal fictions that emphasize the divisive, dissociative relations that neoliberalism requires to operate effectively as a rationality of governance. One of these legal fictions that emerges in the legal cases on assisted dying and is referred to throughout is the "immune person:" this is the individual neoliberal subject who is framed as a "bounded," "immunized" subject of law—a subject who cannot be interfered with by outsiders. The fiction of the immune person is created through the perpetuation of concepts in legal cases on assisted dying that sustain the belief that subjects are neoliberal individuals who are sovereign over themselves (self-directing) and who are private persons. The second of these legal fictions is the "immune society." This is the depiction of a neoliberal society, which is the totality of immune subjects, held in common by their reciprocal dissociation. Legal decisions on assisted dying draw on and create concepts in the legal cases that shape a view that a good and well-operating society is a totality of immunized persons, who are best supported in their individual aims for life by removing barriers that impose positive obligations on said persons and by creating a society where persons do not obligate others.

Immune persons in the immune society are related to one another by virtue of their lack of interference with one another: they are reciprocally immune. Legal cases typically construct appellants as particular kinds of subjects who would impose a positive obligation onto others. Appellants, framed as elderly, disabled and terminally ill, are also framed as subjects who threaten the neoliberal order because they are more of a burden and interfere with the reciprocal freedom and dissociation of others in the immune society. Likewise, appellants also internalize this neoliberal ethos and often seek assisted death through the same concepts and fictions that the law uses to deny them. As the subsequent chapters demonstrate, appeals to die often replicate a neoliberal ethos by invoking legal "rights" and drawing on concepts such as "dignity," "sovereignty" and so on that generate the same fictions that are also potentially divisive, closed off and immunizing. The law, and sometimes appellants themselves, draws on concepts such as enmity, vulnerability, inviolability, security, dignity and dependency to create the fiction of the immune society and immune person: by drawing on vulnerability, for example, and by framing some subjects as dependents, the law operates as a conduit of neoliberalism and feeds fictions of an immune person and immune society that precludes the prospect of some forms of assisted death. This helps explain why certain legal decisions on assisted dying are made possible and others are not: those that are made possible comport with the underpinning political rationality that is able to sustain the fiction of the immune subject and immune society.

The following pages of the book, however, also reveal how this logic of legal fictions might seem odd: why would the law not simply allow practices of assisted dying in order to preserve the immune society per se? We are presented with a certain paradox: on the one hand the neoliberal rationality might be better served if it were to allow the subject, framed as a dependent and burden on other immune persons and the immune society, to die; after all, these subjects are said to interfere with the operation of neoliberalism that demands all subjects are individualized and do not impose on the freedom of other individual subjects. On the other hand the neoliberal rationality seems committed to maintaining the unit of the individual and closing off this individual from the intrusion and interference of others, so the act of assisted death becomes impossible. As will become apparent, it seems that to date a neoliberal political rationality has dealt with this problem as best it can by drawing on or creating concepts that allow some forms of assisted death only if they can be framed in a way that comports with its logic: these acts are rationalized through the use of concepts that feed the legal fiction of the immune person. For instance, Chapter 3 explores how the law will draw on the concept of inviolability to create the fiction of the immune person that will license passive euthanasia as an "omission" and as a form of "letting die" that comports with the neoliberal norm of non-interference. Arguably the English law has yet to find a way to sustain the fiction of the immune person and immune society that would allow the acts of assisted death that current appellants have aimed for; this, however, seems to have been made possible in the recent case of Taylor in *Carter v Canada* (2015).

Exposing the operation of legal fictions emergent in case law on assisted dying, with a particular emphasis on the legal decisions and the arguments put forth from appellants, enables one to reveal how the fictions of the immune person and immune society that both legal decisions that deny assisted dying, and legal appeals in favor of assisted dying, (embedded in the same neoliberal rationality of governance) rely upon and feed an individualistic, uncompassionate and closed-off politics. In framing the problem of assisted dying as a problem of a political ethos that is divisive and closed, one can then begin to rethink a new "affirmative" politics. To be clear, this affirmative politics is not one that simply affirms practices of assisted dying per se: it does not support an outright "liberal" call for a reversal of the current legal decisions in favor of "the right to die" such as those calls noted earlier with reference to the *Philosopher's Brief.* Consideration of this wider socio-political context is important for assisted dying discussions because it breaks with what some ethicists, such as Peter Singer (1994), describe as a "liberalisation" of the law. For instance, where Singer argues that the legal decision on Anthony Bland's "passive" euthanasia case represented a "liberal" legal decision that ought to be celebrated, this book later shows in Chapter 3 how one can instead read the decision in *Bland* as less of an "opening" for law and more of a "closure," because the logic of the legal decision was based on an "immunization" of the subjects involved in the case: a logic of liberalism that continues into its advanced and "neo" liberal forms does not "liberalize" in the sense that it "opens out" the prospect for assisted death but rather it is precisely this liberalization of the law that closes off such a prospect of openness. An affirmative politics that engages with the socio-political logic of law enables one to reveal the fictions that law generates in denying the prospect of assisted dying and in doing so this affirmative politics seeks to shift the way we attempt to conceptualize assisted dying. If the present text frames the problem of assisted dying as a problem of an individualistic and closed-off political ethos, it also frames an affirmative politics as a prospect for a more communal and open political ethos. Speaking of assisted dying as a prospect for community in the affirmative sense does not mean imposing another, albeit different, dogmatic politics, this time replacing a neoliberal individualism with a form of communitarianism. Rather, it implies opening up the concepts and fictions that sustain our relations toward one another in fixed and prescriptive ways that are codified in law; it also means considering what other prospects for assisted dying might arise if we deconstruct these concepts and try to think otherwise. Finally, it means being cautious of apparently "good" liberal outcomes such as the "right to assisted death" if these legal changes, when they appear, remain framed in a closed off, neoliberal divisive and non-relational logic.

In short, the following pages explore how several key concepts emerge to articulate the two key legal fictions described as the "immune person" who is bounded, sovereign and independent from relations with others, and the "immune society" of which these subjects are connected to in their mutual dissociation from one another. These legal fictions in right to die cases enable the law to rule in specific situations as it does: legal fictions emergent in these cases reflect a neoliberal political rationality that is at once individualizing and totalizing, and has a privatizing agenda that pits people competitively against one another. Compassion is not one of its emphasized relations; nor is dependency; nor is relationality more broadly speaking.

Notes

1 See Butler, J. (2012). Adorno Prize Lecture: Can One Lead a Good life in a Bad Life? *Radical Philosophy*: www.egs.edu/faculty/judith-butler/articles/can-one-lead-a-good-life-in-a-bad-life/

2 One might draw a parallel here to Jacques Derrida's notion of the gift, which he understands as an impossible kind of giving (e.g., Weir, 2013). The gift cannot be returned because as soon as the other gives back or owes me, or even is grateful for or recognizes a gift, what I have given him or her "there will not have been a gift;" rather, the gift becomes a matter of economic exchange. "It is perhaps in this sense that the gift is the impossible. Not impossible but *the* impossible" (Derrida, 1991: 7).

3 In his discussion of immunity and community, Esposito (2008, 2010, 2011, 2013) regards the former as the creation of the "proper," while the latter is defined as "improper." Esposito therefore explains that community understood through the concept of *munus* is not based on or forged through something proper that is shared—for example community is not defined by a shared origin of where one comes from, or a shared identity, or the instance that we all "have" a body. All of these things or shared attributes would be something "proper" that defines community.

4 While this book also broaches neoliberalism, and in particular neoliberalism's association with law as one of its central apparatuses or technologies from this

governmental framework, following Foucault and other scholars it continues to use the original term neoliberalism as opposed to Rose's term advanced liberalism to describe this strategy of governance. This is mainly because it is more consistent with other literature drawn that generally refers to neoliberalism.

5 See Brown, W. (2003). "Neo-liberalism and the End of Liberal Democracy," *Theory & Event*, paragraph 38. There are no page numbers for this piece.

6 This significantly departs from an "expulsion thesis on law" (Golder, 2013: 22; Golder and Fitzpatrick, 2009: 24–25; Hunt and Wickham, 1994). Because Foucault had claimed that the juridical model of power was no longer predominant in the West, Alan Hunt and Gary Wickham (1994) questioned whether the law was a "relevant" site through which to investigate how modern mechanisms of power operate. In contrast to this expulsion thesis, others have persuasively argued that even through a Foucaultian theoretical lens, law remains a useful site of scholarly investigation.

7 Smith (2000: 283), for instance, writes that "Expert knowledge occupies a privileged position in government and its essentially discretionary and norm–governed judgments infiltrate and colonise previous sites of power."

8 See for example e.g., Dworkin, 1993; Dworkin *et al.*, 1997; Singer, 1994; Huxtable, 2002.

9 One might consider the varying context between the United States where families have been known to suffer tremendous debt from medical costs, versus countries such as England and Canada where perhaps the financial burden is less important (though the alleged "social" or "emotional" burden might be argued to be equivalent (e.g., Mihic, 2008)).

10 BBC News, 2004: http://news.bbc.co.uk/2/hi/uk_news/4090463.stm

Chapter 2

Vulnerable Persons and Relations of Enmity[1]

Tony Nicklinson was certain that he wanted to end his life, so much so that he noted prior to the hearing of his case in 2012 that "I have wanted my life to end since 2007 so it is not a passing whim ... A decision going against me condemns me to a life of increasing misery" (*R (Nicklinson) v Ministry of Justice* [2012] EWHC 2381 (Admin), (2012) MHLO, paragraph 14). Nicklinson's narrative is well known and was broadcast across the English and international media; he was a formerly active man—a rugby player and an avid skydiver. Following a business trip where he suffered from a devastating stroke, Nicklinson was left paralyzed below the neck and unable to speak. Able to move his head and eyes only, Nicklinson's form of communication had since been through a computer that he controlled through eye blinking. A statement recorded in the judgment on his case shares Nicklinson's thoughts:

> My life can be summed up as dull, miserable, demeaning, undignified and intolerable ... it is misery created by the accumulation of lots of things which are minor in themselves but, taken together, ruin what's left of my life. Things like ... constant dribbling; having to be hoisted everywhere; loss of independence, ... particularly toileting and washing, in fact all bodily functions (by far the hardest thing to get used to); having to forgo favourite foods; ... having to wait until 10:30 to go to the toilet ... in extreme circumstances I have gone in the chair, and have sat there until the carers arrived at the normal time.
>
> (Paragraph 13)

Despite Nicklinson's appeals to be allowed to end his life through voluntary active euthanasia—which would have meant that someone else such as his wife, Jane, or a physician, could have helped him pass—his case was denied in August of 2012. The court report acknowledged that in other countries, such as Switzerland, the right to assisted death had been legalized. However, while England had advanced some laws regarding end of life decisions—for instance, the Suicide Act of 1961 decriminalized individuals who attempted to commit suicide, and a previous case, *Purdy* [2009], set precedent that permitted a loved one to help transport an individual to a place where assisted death was legalized—it did not recognize voluntary active euthanasia as lawful. Nicklinson, who the court recognized could not end his own life (other than through self-starvation), required the assistance of another, and this assistance would remain an act that would not immune from criminal conviction (*R (Nicklinson) v Ministry of Justice* [2012] EWHC 2381 (Admin), (2012) MHLO, paragraph 15).

Although a number of advocates for Nicklinson's position have advanced forms of appeal, including Lord Joffe who has presented Parliament with several amended bills regarding the right to die, English law appears to be bound to the belief that voluntary euthanasia—which in this case seems to have been conflated with the term "mercy killing" to encompass the notion of a "consented death"—should in no way be decriminalized. Instead, the law stipulates that the actor who ends a life is inevitably a "murderer," regardless of whether the act was committed in full accord: "It has been established for centuries," stated the Court, "that consent to the deliberate infliction of death is no defence to a charge of murder" (Paragraph 57, s.7). The judge argued that the relation between mercy "killing," voluntary euthanasia and murder was "inevitable."

Canada's Sue Rodriguez's case raised many similar points concerning the association between assisted death and murder. Justice McLachlin's dissenting voice stipulated that the assenting opinion of Justice Sopinka denied assisted dying due to the latter's belief that any "active participation by one individual in the death of another is intrinsically morally and legally wrong" (*Rodriguez v British Columbia* (Attorney General) [1993] 3 S.C.R. 519: 601, paragraph 209). McLachlin noted in turn that this blind belief in, and universalization of, the moral depravity that one suffers (and that a community suffers) when one takes the life of another has justified the blanket "prohibition on assisted suicide…because the state has an interest in absolutely criminalizing any willful act which contributes to the death of another" (Paragraph 209). But why does the law respond in such an "absolute" way, as McLachlin notes here? Why is it that the "mercy killer" is inevitably framed as a murderer when such a death is namely consented to and desired on the basis of claims to compassion?

Enemies and the Proper

Patrick Hanafin's (2007, 2009) work on legal cases concerning the beginning of life is salient here. His analysis of "right to life" legal cases in Italy noted—albeit in passing reference—how the law constructed a concept of enmity to rationalize legal restrictions placed on in vitro fertilization. In particular, the tenuous grounds upon which Italian law dealt with the question of the legal status of the embryo concerned Hanafin. He asked how Italy, which considers itself a nominally liberal pluralist state, had negotiated its Catholic culturalist underpinnings within its legal structure. The passing of a new act in 2004 that regulated assisted reproductive technology (ART) was particularly contentious. This act stipulated, quite contrary to the Constitution of the Italian Republic, that the embryo had legal rights (to life and to protection) independently of the mother. Hanafin noted that the Catholic Church played a significant role in shaping this act, such that it employed the embryo "as a weapon in the war" against what it called a "culture of death" (Hanafin, 2007: 6).

Most interesting for the present discussion is the notion that this act not only articulated the embryo as a sovereign entity within law (or, established it at the very least as a "potential" sovereign), but also that the law established this sovereign status of the embryo by constituting the mother as a necessary *enemy* of this "embryonic sovereign." The mother was thus conceived as a monstrous other who threatened the embryo's life (Hanafin, 2007: 99).[2] But why did the law rely on an articulation of enmity? What does this reference to enmity in Hanafin's example of a right to life case tell us about how enmity operates as a concept in right to die appeals?

By perpetuating the belief that we are all enemies of one another—that "man is wolf to man" and therefore that we should fear death at the hands of the other—the law appeared to assert its authority as the necessary protector and guarantor of life. In the case of assisted dying, this appeared to occur by framing compassionate death in the context of a criminal act whereby the other is always, inevitably, a "murderer." In doing so the law invoked the concept of enmity to feed a legal fiction of an immune person (in this case Nicklinson) whom law must protect from all of those who exist outside of him or herself.

In Nicklinson's case, law deferred to an existing precedent to make this point. It argued the relation between mercy "killing," voluntary euthanasia and murder was "inevitable." The legal case clearly outlined a link between mercy killing and the notion of a bellicose relationship with the other. This warlike relation was defined through the historical legal example of the duel: "this proposition is established beyond doubt by the law on dueling, where even if the deceased was the challenger, his consent to the risk of being deliberately killed by his opponent does not alter the case" (*R (Nicklinson) v Ministry of Justice* [2012] EWHC 2381 (Admin), (2012) MHLO, paragraph 57, s.7).

The duel, deemed analogous to mercy killing in Nicklinson's court judgment, might prompt some sort of response here. Dueling was deemed analogous because it replicated a scenario in which even if a person consented to his or her own death, the person who committed the consented act was not exonerated. Drawing on the duel by way of example enabled the law to cultivate an image of two subjects embedded in a "theatrical presentation" of power, or a war-like "event" (Foucault, 2003: 92); it constructed subjects as enemies of one another.

The Commission in Nicklinson's case also deferred to a precedent set in the case of *Re A (Children) (Conjoined Twins Surgical Separation)* 2 WLR 480, [2000]; this provided another example whereby case law drew on concepts of enmity and vulnerability to feed a legal fiction of an immune person who the law would "protect" and defend from a necessary enemy. Nicklinson's case drew on *Re A* as an example in which death (i.e. killing) was deemed acceptable when granted "in favour of life" (Paragraph 70). In *Re A*, twins, Jodie and Mary, were born conjoined. Mary was reliant on an artery that connected her to Jodie; however, she would not survive as a singleton. If doctors did not separate the twins, neither would survive, but if they did separate them Mary's life would inevitably be lost. The ruling concluded that the twins could be separated and, ultimately, that Mary's life could be "let go" for the sake of saving Jodie. The case had pleaded that the doctors were "coming to Jodie's defence and removing her from the threat of fatal harm to her presented by Mary's draining her life blood" (*Nicklinson v MOJ*, 2012, paragraph 70). Even though this case dealt with two newborn twins, who would typically be regarded as innocent, the law invoked the concepts of enmity and vulnerability to articulate its decision. It argued that Jodie suffered by virtue of a fear of her twin "draining her life blood" (7.7). Mary directly threatened the life of her sister. The law invoked the concept of enmity when it articulated the decision to allow the death of one twin, who was an enemy, to save the other twin, who was vulnerable, on the basis of "self-defence." The law constructed Mary as Jodie's enemy. The decision to allow Mary's death through self-defense to protect Jodie fed a fiction of Jodie as an immune person who was merely protected from the threat Mary posed.

From the onset one might question this relationship between self-defense and the legal appeal to life and to death. To what extent are these two things related? The Commission in Nicklinson's case drew on self-defense to articulate when it would be deemed acceptable for a subject to take the life of another subject; however, it does seem somewhat peculiar that in an instance of two conjoined twin babies the law appeared to rationalize its decision to kill one on the basis that the other twin appeared to be a threat and an enemy. As with Hanafin's example of the monstrous mother, the articulation of the concept of enmity seems to figure as a central tool to feed the fiction of the immune person who must be protected from all others whom he or she would otherwise fear as a direct threat to his or her life.

Law as Norm

The law operating as a discourse and technology of governance also operates as a norm: the law seems to be able to use concepts of enmity and vulnerability to articulate legal fictions around the life that it chooses to protect. It could have sought to protect Mary as an immune person, but instead it used vulnerability and enmity to articulate her as a threat to Jodie. Likewise, it was not simply that Mary threatened Jodie in the sense that she threatened her life; Mary also obligated Jodie. Mary could not be articulated as an immune person because she drew from Jodie's lifeblood; she could not live independently, on her own, as her own immune person within an immune society that respected the immunity of other persons (i.e. Jodie).

We can see a shared logic in this case of *Re A (Children) (Conjoined Twins Surgical Separation)* that is echoed in the case of Nicklinson: despite compassionate motives established for killing in the latter's case, and despite the desire from the subject himself to die at the hands of a trusted other, the law responded by calling upon a precedent that invoked a rationalization of the other as necessarily an enemy. In Nicklinson's and Rodriguez's cases, the association of the act of taking life with unlawful murder as if this were "inevitable" is arguably curious. In assisted dying cases, this inevitable association occurs by framing compassionate killing in the context of a criminal act whereby the other is always, inevitably, a "murderer." As I have noted elsewhere (Hardes, 2013, 2014), this "inevitability" of judgment is at the heart of Esposito's critique of immunization. Governance mechanisms are able to immunize subjects from one another by deciding on a guilty verdict in advance of an act, "regardless of whether the circumstances merit it"

(Esposito, 2011: 32). Law fixes subjects as enemies of one another in order to ensure these enemies are known in advance; law must be able to make enemies known to one another such that legal fictions of immune persons and an immune society can claim to protect subjects from these enemies. As Esposito (2011: 32) notes: "Life is not condemned because it is guilty but in order to make it guilty." If the "stated aim of law is to preserve life ... life can be preserved only if held in the fold of an inexorable anticipation that judges life to be guilty even before any of its acts can be judged" (Esposito, 2011: 32–33). The central point here is that the law must create truths about human nature through concepts such as enmity that feed legal fictions in order to judge some forms of humanity as guilty and condemn an act before it has even been performed.

Deferring to examples such as the vampiric twins and dueling in case law when dealing with the prospect of assisted dying are two instances in which we see the law create legal fictions of the immune person (that is, the bounded, individual, person protected from what exists outside himself or herself) and the immune society (i.e. the totality of immune persons). Law used the concepts of enmity and vulnerability in ways that sustained and fed these fictions by generating beliefs about the possible limits of human relationships that required "shoring up" by reifying a binary between friend and foe. Within a regime of governance that advances the values of liberal individualism—that is, freedom of self-determination, and therefore an individual "sovereignty over oneself" of sorts—an immune person—the law appears to need to cultivate the notion that one's neighbor is to be feared through recourse to the "essence" of human nature as wolf-like. This is akin to the governmental approach to "conducting conduct" that Foucault (1991a) had noted whereby the concept of enmity is articulated in order to perpetuate a particular truth of human relationships, which in turn rationalizes the legal fiction of the immune person, and also rationalizes the fiction of the immune society, both of which operate through legal divisions between subjects on the basis of knowable behavioral "traits" and a particular "anthropology" of humankind (e.g., Joronen, 2013; Read, 2009). Nicklinson's case also reveals this point:

> recognizing a partial excuse of acting out of compassion would be dangerous. Just as a defence of necessity 'can very simply become a mask for anarchy', so the concept of 'compassion'—vague in itself—could very easily become a cover for selfish or ignoble

> reasons for killing, not least because people often act out of mixed motives.
>
> (*R (Nicklinson) v Ministry of Justice* [2012] EWHC 2381 (Admin), (2012) MHLO, paragraph 54, s7.7)

Thomas Hobbes and Carl Schmitt also noted this necessary deferral to the concept of enmity that defined man's essence to legitimate a legal fiction of an immune society. Their fictive immune society operated through sovereign rationality that divided subjects reciprocally from one another on the basis that subjects were part of a totality of immune persons who could not be trusted. Sovereignty emerged as a political mechanism of protection that demanded "a pessimistic anthropology, which has a vision of man as bad, corrupt, dangerous, fearful and violent" (Derrida, 2009: 44) in order to ground and legitimate itself. Derrida (2009) has written on this aspect of Hobbes and Schmitt's theorizing: he recognized, like them, how sovereignty politics relied on deferrals to the belief that human nature is wolf-like and that we are all enemies of one another in order to legitimate itself as a mode of governance by creating the unit of the individual immune person who is part of an immune totality. We see here emerging in this discussion of sovereignty the same underpinning logic; it operates on the same basis of an individualizing and totalizing logic sustained through fictions of an immune individual and an immune society which is a totality of immune individuals.

Continuing with Hobbes's sovereignty as an instance of immunization, Esposito further describes this relation between protection and the constitution of the proper. When we are brought into "unity" with one another under the sovereign contract we are not brought into relation as friends, but instead we remain enemies. In being brought together in unity under the immune mechanism, we are held in a certain non-relation (Hardes, 2014). Thus, he writes:

> The relation that unites men [through immunization] does not pass between friend and enemy and not even between enemy and friend, but between enemy and enemy, given that every temporary friendship is instrumental ... with regard to managing the only social bond possible, namely enmity.
>
> (Esposito, 2010: 27)

In short, the immunity mechanism of sovereignty did not offer us protection that would allow us to live in relational harmony with one another as friends but rather, through immunization, it brought us into what he calls "reciprocal dissociation" or a "unity without relation" (Esposito, 2010: 28). This is also why Esposito suggests the immunization mechanism both totalizes us and divides us from one another. Without this recourse to man's nature as corrupt or bad and something to be feared, we might question the very role of law and legal sanctions. The friend/foe distinction underpins and sustains law as a mechanism of protection (Esposito, 2008). With reference to case law on assisted dying one might note that the law seems to discursively establish itself as a mechanism of protection of individuals through the construction of compassionate cases as inevitably sinister.

It is not simply under sovereign regimes of governance that this kind of immunizing mechanism operates. Through political rationalities of liberalism (Esposito, 2008), and increasingly neoliberalism (Campbell, 2011), we witness an intensification of immunization mechanisms. The "totality" of sovereignty is, like the totality of neoliberalism, only a totality in the sense that it is a society of immune persons protected from one another. The state of being immune, which we so "enjoy" to this present day, can be summarized by the de Tocquevillian adage whereby we live "side by side unconnected by a common tie" (Esposito, 2008: 76); this maxim has arguably become an even more pertinent under neoliberal rationalities of governance that continue to shape subjects in ways that are increasingly divisive (May, 2012; Olssen, 2010).

Speaking to the prospect of solidarity that might break from the individualizing tendencies of immunization more generally and neoliberal immunization more specifically, Todd May (2012: 135) adds to this conversation: "Because of the individualizing tendency of neoliberalism we often find it difficult to think in terms of solidarity ... we don't possess ways of thinking in terms of solidarity, because we are discouraged from thinking these ways." Solidarity and other reciprocal and relational concepts are unable to emerge on the very basis that borders have been shored up between "the same (of friendship) and the other (of enmity)" (May, 2012: 135). It is the constitution of and perpetuation of the concept of enmity that plays a role in creating legal fictions of immune persons and an immune society that makes this reciprocally dissociative relation between immune persons possible.

Vulnerability

Emerging in association with enmity in right to die legal appeals is also that of vulnerability. This concept transpires most prominently in the recent 2013 case of *Fleming v Ireland & Ors*, Judgment, I EHC 2, [2013] in which Marie Fleming, the appellant, requested an assisted death. In this case vulnerability emerges in association with a concept of burden in order to frame a symbolic type of enmity.

It is important to contextualize Fleming's case because it overlaps with a decision made (and discussions thereof) in the 2012 Canadian appeal from Gloria Taylor. The judge of the latter case, Justice Lynn Smith, had been the first in Canadian and English law to consider the right to assisted death favorably. In her decision she granted Taylor a constitutional exemption that allowed Taylor the right to seek physician assisted death within a year while Parliament could take steps to reconsider legislation on the matter. Taylor's case considered whether the appellants, were they to remain alive, would necessarily internalize a belief that they would burden loved ones. The law considered whether assisted death could be legalized on the basis of this internalization of burden; after all, the law argued that subjects seeking death due to a fear of becoming a burden on others would always pose a potential risk for vulnerable persons. Indeed, in other cases like *Rodriguez*, judges had claimed that appellants were vulnerable and required protection from law because even if they outwardly seemed to appeal to die on their own accord the appellant might instead do so out of a fear of burdening family members. However, in her judicial decision Justice Smith ruled out the concern that Taylor had internalized a belief that she was a burden on her family, and therefore ruled out the argument that this internalized burden would coerce Taylor into seeking an assisted death that she might not otherwise have desired (*Carter v Canada* (Attorney General), [2012] BCSC 886). Smith's recognition of Taylor's appeal was reinforced through the most recent Canadian Supreme Court decision that granted Taylor the right to die (*Carter v Canada (Attorney General)*, 2015 SCC5). As the case noted, "vulnerability can be assessed on an individual basis" (paragraph 1) without having to impose a blanket notion of vulnerability which would be attached to an assumption about the appellant being a particular kind of person who ought to indeed feel vulnerable.

In direct response to Justice Smith's ruling, Ireland's Justice Nicholas Kearns articulated his own position on this prospect of burden and coercion in Fleming's case. Kearns provided "evidence" that the threat of burden was still an ever-present possibility; on account of this he dismissed Fleming's appeal to die. Kearns' judgment summary notes:

> The evidence from other countries shows that the risks of abuse are all too real and cannot be dismissed as speculative or distant. One real risk attending such liberalisation is that even with the most rigorous system of legislative checks and safeguards, it would be impossible to ensure that the aged, the disabled, the poor, the unwanted, the rejected, the lonely, the impulsive, the financially compromised and emotionally vulnerable would not avail of this option in order to avoid a sense of being a burden on their family and society. The safeguards built into any liberalised system would, furthermore, be vulnerable to laxity and complacency and might well prove difficult or even impossible to police adequately.
>
> (*Fleming v Ireland & Ors*, Judgment, I EHC 2, 2013)

Not only did the case summary constitute Fleming as a vulnerable subject, but it also constituted her vulnerability in relation to the conditions of enmity and immunity. Kearns argued that right to die appellants would conceive of themselves as burdens due to the direct pressure they would place on their families and caregivers. To support this claim he drew on what one witness, Professor George, called "care fatigue" whereby:

> as a clinician treating patients in the final stages of their lives I have come across it in the most loving family environments. It is easy in such circumstances for seriously ill people to feel a sense of obligation to remove themselves from the scene.
>
> (*Fleming v Ireland & Ors*, Judgment, paragraph 66)

While the concept of enmity may not appear to be immediately apparent in this case, it is implicit in the rationale through concepts of burden and vulnerability. These concepts feed both legal fictions discussed earlier—the fiction of the immune person and the fiction of the immune society. On the one hand, George's statement noted above rationalized the tenets of a neoliberal political rationality that requires good subjects to be self-responsible and not to burden the freedom of others. Here we see the concepts of burden and enmity frame the legal fiction of the immune person—this time, feeding a fiction of the family members as the immune persons who require protecting from Fleming who would be a burden and "enemy" in the sense that she would infringe on the freedom of her loved ones (hence, causing them "care fatigue") (Glasgow, 2012).

This reference to self-responsibility is typically associated with neoliberal governance rationalities that push individuals to take care of themselves (Brown, 2005; Glasgow, 2012; May, 2012; Olssen, 2010). On the other hand the statement from George also rationalized the need to protect and immunize Fleming from the possibility—indeed, the inevitability—that this care fatigue would lead to a state of tension or a "war" of the household, thus coercing Fleming into desiring a death out of fear and obligation. In a political climate in which care is frequently pushed onto families of individuals to remove the burden from the state (Larner, 2000), arguably Fleming's case set in motion new ways that enmity could get introduced as a rationale for increased legal "protection" (or "immunization"), which penetrates law to protect us, even when we do not desire it, from those often deemed most "close" to us: our loved ones.

In this instance, the concept of self-responsibility fed a fiction of Fleming as an immune person and independent subject: she was framed as an immune person, since she ought to be self responsible; however, her immune person status was simultaneously called into question as the concepts of burden and vulnerability framed her as someone who could not take care of herself as an immune person and who would unavoidably and necessarily impose herself onto others. This framed her as an enemy of others (and of the neoliberal immune society itself) but also as a vulnerable requestor who, because of her enemy status, needed protecting from the immune community of individuals that she would otherwise burden and that would then become her enemy.

Nicklinson's case also realized this problematic of vulnerability as it operated alongside legal protection from the constitutive enemy who was alleged to deliver harm. As Nicklinson clearly stated:

> By all means protect the vulnerable. By vulnerable I mean those who cannot make decisions for themselves just don't include me. I am not vulnerable, I don't need help or protection from death or those who would help me. If the legal consequences were not so huge i.e. life imprisonment, perhaps I could get someone to help me. As things stand, I can't get help.
>
> (*R (Nicklinson) v Ministry of Justice* [2012] EWHC 2381 (Admin), (2012) MHLO, paragraph 3)

Writing in the context of restorative justice, Pavlich (2002) notes the problematic uptake of ethical arguments used to defend certain legal decisions. In the context of the discussion of vulnerability this is particularly pertinent. Pavlich argues that ethical claims such as those said to "protect" the vulnerable "operate in the name of supposedly universal principles of harm, or absolute conceptions of general community interests" (Pavlich, 2002: 5). For him, this assumption is damaging because it does not allow us to "seek out ways to envisage entirely new forms of social life" (Pavlich, 2002: 5). It also narrows the very possibilities for considering what indeed constitutes "harm" or, in this case, to consider what we imagine by vulnerability. In the instance of right to die appeals, this commentary is absolutely germane: one must surely note the ways that a law based on an uptake of the concept of vulnerability that claims to be an ethical universal norm reflecting community interests instead does much damage to many members of this community who do not subscribe to the same account. Those persons appealing to the right to die such as Nicklinson certainly do not consider themselves within the same universal context of vulnerability, nor do they wish to be considered thus. Indeed, rather than considering themselves vulnerable to other persons, whom the law establishes as proper enemies that it claims to protect them from, right to die appellants such as Nicklinson instead typically articulate themselves as being vulnerable to the law itself that they claim sentences them to a fate worse than death: a life of inescapable suffering. Not only does Nicklinson's statement give us insight into the problematic that Pavlich (2002) outlines above, but also it speaks more specifically to the implications of law acting as a discourse and technology of a neoliberal political rationality that divides subjects from one another. By perpetuating the concept of vulnerability that feeds the fiction of the immune person who is a proper type of person (a vulnerable person) who inevitably requires protection, this protection is grounded in a division that reflects and sustains the particular logic of the political rationality itself.

Despite the relatively different ways that the cases of Nicklinson, Rodriguez and Fleming invoked the concept of enmity, each fed a necessary "immunization" of life that forged artificial parameters around the self and other. Law's construction of the presence of a possible enemy (either a direct enemy or the enemy of the community that had pressured persons to die in particular ways), was necessary to constitute the fiction of the immune person as an enunciation of a divisive neoliberal ethos. The creation of enemies and vulnerable requestors had the effect of fixing subjects and also fixing the kinds of relations subjects could have with one another. There was no other way of conceiving of society and persons other than as individuals who must be protected and divided from one another; the prospect of assisted dying could not be brought to bear because it was compromised by the very "fact" articulated through legal fictions that human subjects required protection from one another and acts of compassionate killing could not be recognized within this ethos of governance.

On the other side of this divide, however, we must also ask in what ways the refusal of vulnerability, such as Nicklinson's claim that he was not vulnerable, and the depiction of law as a mechanism of communal force or violence imposed on subjects might also be considered complicit with another type of immunizing function, this time by way of the articulation of legal rights themselves. In Nicklinson's case we see a simultaneous rejection of the fiction of the immune person and a reinstatement of it. This presents a paradox. On the one hand he rejects his immune person because he rejects the surrounding concept of enmity that shores it up (i.e. he rejects the idea that others want to kill him for maleficent reasons); on the other hand he brings the immune person back into being because he asserts himself as a bordered, proper subject who is self-directing and self-responsible, and who can make his own decisions independently of others.

Judith Butler (2004) challenges the rejection of vulnerability as a way to establish and legitimate a violent self-centered subject. Although the subject she speaks of is very different (specifically that of the nation state) her insights are still pertinent. According to Butler, when the state denies its vulnerability it effectively erects boundaries and defensive apparatuses around itself. In many ways one could also argue that the rights claims of appellants themselves do the same: by denying their vulnerability the appellants erect boundaries and defensive apparatuses around themselves. In doing so they actively construct the enmity of the other—hence the law itself or the community of persons who seek to deny assisted dying—and they also construct their own sovereignty as a self-directing, individual subject. Butler describes this violent, self-centered subject in the following way:

> Its actions constitute the building of a subject that seeks to restore and maintain its mastery through the systematic destruction of its multilateral relations ... It shores itself up, seeks to reconstitute its imagined wholeness, but only at the price of denying its own vulnerability, its dependency, its exposure, where it exploits those very features in others, thereby making those features "other to" itself.
>
> (Butler, 2004: 41)

Derrida (2009) notes a similar point regarding the liberal individual who attempts to immunize him or herself against the violence of the state. "There are different and sometimes antagonistic forms of sovereignty, and it is always in the name of one that one attacks the other", he writes (Derrida, 2009: 76). One might thus recognize how subjective appeals to the right to die, particularly as they refuse a status of vulnerability, are not neutral or innocent but are also embedded in the shared neoliberal political rationality that serves to close off the borders around the self. One must therefore consider how such liberal rights appeals also, to some degree, aim to fix a "proper" subject through constituting a legal fiction of an immune person (Hardes, 2014). Liberal right to die appeals that deny vulnerability and appropriate this idea of a self-directing subjectivity might be considered complicit in constituting a subjectivity that appears to be complete and also defended from the other as an alleged enemy (Mihic, 2008).

Upon noting this centrality, indeed necessity, of enmity it becomes clearer as to why the law denies the prospect of compassionate killing. The reason lies here: law does not seem to recognize compassion as a motive given that the concept of compassion would contradict the political rationality that depends on a particular legal fiction of a reciprocally dissociated society shored up by an anthropology of humanity as self-serving, self-sufficient and properly individual. In Nicklinson's case, the Commission interestingly posits this "problem" of mercy killing as it relates to compassion:

> Under the current law, the compassionate motives of the "mercy" killer are in themselves never capable of providing a basis for a partial excuse. Some would say that this is unfortunate. On this view, the law affords more recognition to other less, or at least no more, understandable emotions such as anger (provocation), and fear (self-defence).
>
> (*R (Nicklinson) v Ministry of Justice* [2012] EWHC 2381 (Admin), (2012) MHLO, paragraph 54, s7.7)

This passage highlights two important, interrelated points. First, it identifies that "compassion," framed as a more positive virtue, is not recognized in law. Second, it contrasts this compassionate motive to less virtuous reasons for ending a life that are framed in terms of fear and anger. Thus, the Commission recognizes how "lesser emotions" or negative precepts like anger and fear can be considered acceptable motives for the taking of a life that lessen a conviction from murder to "manslaughter." For instance, acting out of a fear for one's life can be considered self-defense and therefore not murder of the first degree (*R*

(Nicklinson) v Ministry of Justice [2012] EWHC 2381 (Admin), (2012) MHLO, paragraph 54, s7.7). Likewise, arguing that one was "provoked" into action that led to another's death also acquires a reduced sentence. However, in England and Canada[3] acting out of "compassion" does not exonerate subjects or grant them a status of "manslaughter" but instead labels subjects as "murderers."

Making "Proper" Subjects

Following Esposito's political project as well as the insights that Campbell (2011) has added, we can explain in more detail the challenge that both scholars extend to the creation of proper subjects (what I am describing as a fiction of an immune person) that establishes us as reciprocally dissociated from one another (as another fiction, the immune society) and confines us to "defensive barriers" that enclose the self. This enclosure, which occurs through concepts that feed legal fictions and is arguably most rife in the contemporary neoliberal context, is what creates the appearance of someone who is "proper;" hence, it creates the fiction of the immune person who appears as an individual sovereign subject and an "absolute" or "indivisible" self (Derrida, 2009). As previously noted, the concepts of enmity and vulnerability that operate through the discourse of law as a technology of a neoliberal rationality of governance feed this fiction. We can thus say that law, operating as a discourse and a technology of a neoliberal rationality of governance, articulates the concepts of enmity and vulnerability to legitimate legal decisions through the creation of legal fictions that forge a separation between a "proper" self and a "proper" other, of which this proper self and proper other is part of a proper totality of proper selves. The establishment of the proper subject (the legal fiction of the immune person) is necessary in order for law to fix its target (i.e. fix persons into the categories of vulnerable and/or the enemy) and make a decision (Naffine, 2009; Pavlich, 2013).

However, in forging proper subjects of law, which is necessary for a legal judgment to be made, the constitution of the "proper" also closes us off to the possibility of a relational ethics (Campbell, 2011). "Otherness" itself is central to this proper constitution: the other must be a "proper" other, which is, ultimately, a "known" other. Moreover, this other is "made known" as an "other" by calling on concepts that frame and fix what is proper to it: its status as an enemy or as a vulnerable subject. In the same way that Esposito noted that life must be determined as guilty in order to found law itself, we could say the same about the way that concepts and fictions operate in order to already define and fix a particular anthropology of humanity that legitimates legal decisions to deny assisted dying. The subject of the right to die—the appellant—must be made known as both a vulnerable subject and as an enemy such that he or she can be brought within law's sphere and judged accordingly. Likewise, the subject who would otherwise help the appellant to die must also be made known before an act of killing even occurs such that he or she can be labeled and judged as guilty. In the cases presented we see how the other or enemy is made known. For instance, Hanafin's embryonic sovereign could only be granted a proper status by making known an enemy that constituted it as a proper subject: its negative relation to the mother gave it a property and made it a subject. To thwart Nicklinson's appeal to the right to die, a known other, an enemy, had to be created. Despite no obvious enemy, Nicklinson's case required an artificial enemy to rationalize a denial of his appeal: the law invoked the legal status of "murderer" to directly constitute the other through this "known" lens, without even demanding a performance of the "murderous" act. In this regard we can claim that law rationalizes its decisions on denying assisted dying through the construction of concepts that allow law to fix its gaze by creating legal fictions of proper subjects of law (Naffine, 2009; Pavlich, 2012a, 2012b).

Despite the law's perpetuation of these concepts grounded in a neoliberal rationality of governance that feed fictions of the immune person and immune society, these concepts and fictions, like their larger supporting rationality, are not "truths" per se. Legal decisions on the right to die merely serve to fix and reify human relationships as necessarily immunized and divided from one another by bringing into effect these concepts of enmity and vulnerability that feed divisive and dissociative, individualizing and totalizing legal fictions. As Foucault (1989) notes, governmentality operates through a "conduct of conduct;" it shapes subjectivities through a fabrication of social conditions. Governmentality may be seen here to operate through law by using concepts of enmity and vulnerability to place limits on the prospects of acceptable human relationships through legal judgments that comport with the defining rationality of governance.

Esposito says something similar about the operation of enmity as part of his account of immunization and the way that immunization mechanisms close off the self from others. He notes, for instance, the "mythic" idea of enmity. This appeal to myth is akin to Derrida's claim that sovereignty is only ever a "performance" (Derrida, 2009: 28). From Esposito's vantage, concepts and fictions that enunciate political rationalities of governance that operate on the basis of the need to divide subjects from one another do so with the goal of presenting these divisions as natural and necessary: they do so through the establishment of a war-like division between subjects that is grounded in a defense of the individual self, as we have seen articulated in legal cases where the other is articulated as an enemy of the self. Yet, such war-like states are governance mechanisms that "make known" the enemy and, as such, rely on a static division between self and other (Esposito, 2011: 159). He or she who is other (the enemy) can be identified clearly, and this known enemy can be defeated. The concept of enmity makes possible the legal rationalization of denying assisted dying by making known the other (as a proper subject), and immunizing the subject from this other absolutely: "With the corpses of the enemies removed or reused for exercises," Esposito (2011: 159) writes, "… the battlefield has now been cleared. The body has regained its integrity: once immunized, it can no longer be attacked by an enemy."

Rather than being regarded as "immortal" and "final", this division of subjects and the immunization of subjects from one another is a process embedded with "structural aporias" (Esposito, 2011: 159). Immunity is not a mechanism of absolute closure, despite invoking concepts and fictions that make it appear as such; rather, the closing off of the self from the other, which is articulated as a part of human nature within the contemporary context, must be read from Esposito's vantage as something that can always, and will always, open back up to the prospect of more relational ways of being in common. For Esposito this is so given the intimate relation of immunity (or the closure and appropriation of the self) with community that is bound to an originary dependency that we share with one another in the *munus*.

In his reflections on neoliberalism, communitarian scholar Mark Olssen (2010: 174) also notes that a neoliberal governmentality tends to forge closures around subjects through the constitution of proper human relationships by attempting to promote ideals of "self-reliance … responsibilization … and an enterprise culture." However, he notes that this detracts from the ways that we are intimately bound together through a shared dependency that at base shapes our human relationships. He writes, for instance, that, "dependency is, in effect, a part of interconnectedness, or relationality, by which our lives are defined by our commitments to others" (Olssen, 2010: 174).

Having identified this problem of neoliberalism, Olssen also suggests that there are always other ways of thinking moving forward. This condition of division, immunization and the proper can always be reversed to an opening toward other ways of being in common that are grounded in ideas of solidarity, community and mutual dependency. This is what Esposito (2010) finds in his concept of *munus*. This is also what might be considered as an opening up of the defensive borders around the notion of self, and a deconstruction of these borders in order to imagine other ways of being that are more in tune with the interconnectedness of the human condition. Indeed, once we have revealed the way that the "proper" is forged we can in turn critique and deconstruct it. For instance, we can deconstruct as we have done how proper subjects are constituted through a legal mechanism of "protection" that unequivocally closes off our relations to the other by defining this other as one's absolute enemy, despite the appeal to this other for help at the end of life. Likewise, one might posit in the same vein that creating an artificial mode of protection around an embryo, which forges its proper status in opposition to a known enemy that is its mother, is another insidious cruelty that disregards the very relationality of life, or the relationality of the "subject."

This depiction of the operational features of a neoliberal political rationality and law's generation of legal fictions that are enunciations of this rationality by way of law's creation of the proper subject (immune person and immune society) may be used to highlight how immunity does the "work" of conservative discourses that frame the mother as an enemy of the fetus, thus rationalizing Christian, Catholic and right-wing beliefs. Likewise, in the context of assisted dying one might consider how conservative discourses could enunciate mechanisms of immunization to err on the side of life that frames any other (besides God) who takes life as interfering with the theological order. However, it is important to note that this proper status of the subject is equally used to do the work of "liberal democratic" politics, for instance from the vantage of "liberal" right to die appeals. In this regard, the constitution of the proper subject has implications for both sides of the political debate. The key problem in both cases is the attempt to close off relations between subjects through the insistence on concepts that feed legal fictions that are grounded in divisive mechanisms of immunity and the proper, particularly when law utilizes a lexicon of war to construct enmity in order to articulate the individual "self" in modern politics. Just as conservative discourses that draw on the concept of enmity are dangerous, so, too, can liberal democratic discourses slip when they rely on and inculcate legal fictions of "proper" subjects who are immune persons within an immune and reciprocally dissociative totality.

Enmity and Vulnerability for the Sake of Immunity

Understanding how legal cases articulate concepts of enmity and vulnerability that feed legal fictions to help enunciate a neoliberal ethos can help us rearticulate a politics of assisted dying. Concepts of enmity and vulnerability work within legal fictions of the immune person and immune society that shore up the limits of human relationships in two ways. The first is through law's articulation of the subject who would help the person die as necessarily an "other" by fixing the gaze on them as performing an act of murder without considering other motives for taking life. This fixes the appellant as vulnerable and the assister as an enemy: it creates the legal fiction of the proper immune person. The second is through the appellant's right to die appeal itself, which also does not escape this problematic. The appellant's articulation of the right to die through law, by refusing vulnerability and claiming instead to assert self-direction and self-sovereignty, also conforms to the shared neoliberal rationality of governance that operates on the basis that subjects are able to take care of themselves, that they can be self sufficient individual subjects, and that they therefore conform to the social conditions in which they find themselves shaped as subjects (Mihic, 2008). In short, the appeal itself also feeds the legal fiction of the immune person. In this sense, one can ask to what extent rights claims also shore up the limits of human relationships whereby in appealing to the prospect of assisted death subjects are also paradoxically asking the law to immunize them and forge them through a fiction as immune persons.

Moreover, as we have seen, law uses concepts of enmity and vulnerability not only to forge fictions of the immune person, but also to forge the immune society in which persons are a part. For instance, Fleming's case highlights how the concepts of burden and vulnerability also feed a fiction of a society that demands subjects are self-responsible and self-sufficient and that each subject can operate as a fully immune person within the totality: one must not obligate or impose oneself onto other immune persons; otherwise one becomes articulated as an enemy: enmity gets invoked to shore up the immune person of others (family members) and reinforces the immune society as that which needs protecting.

Neither of these positions—the law's denial of assisted death, or the right to die appeal itself—necessarily challenges the conditions of a neoliberal governmentality that relies on a legal fiction of immune persons divided from one another to live freely in a totality of reciprocal dissociation: neither position challenges the way that law divides or immunizes subjects from one another through the generation of concepts and fictions that are reflective of neoliberal governance rationalities; rather, both positions are fixed within a rationality that continues to erect borders around the self and shores up human relational limits through compliance with, and indeed generation of, fictions through remaining wedded to the articulation of concepts that feed these fictions. The question then becomes: how can we imagine an affirmative politics of assisted dying without relying on concepts of enmity and vulnerability that feed legal fictions that constitute the "proper" subject as he or she who is in need of protection from an adversarial other? Or, perhaps better put, how might we envisage a more "relational" ethics that notes, and works against, the performative features of these utterances of the "absolute enemy", the vulnerable subject and the "proper" more broadly conceived?

This chapter has shown how the law creates concepts and fictions that divide us from one another to create a politics that closes us off from one another. As this book continues to argue throughout, this closing off of subjectivities is problematic because it closes us off as defensive selves and dismisses a more relational ethic (Campbell, 2011; May, 2012; Olssen, 2010). Despite the use of the concept of enmity to fix subjects through immunity's protective enclaves, the "other" who is constituted as this enemy is not strictly an "other" but instead is always reciprocally related to us. A more relational ethic would not close us off from one another through mechanisms of immunization and it would not fix subjects as necessary enemies and vulnerable subjects; instead it would deconstruct these subject positions.

Considering the various ways this chapter has shown how the law uses concepts to fix subject positions that allow it to feed its legal fictions, the next chapter explores another emergent concept within the legal cases that is also used to feed legal fictions of the immune person and the immune society: this concept is "inviolability" of the subject, particularly as it is used to feed the fiction of the immune person who is an inviolable person.

Notes

1 An earlier version of this chapter is published as Hardes, J. (2014). Biopolitics and the enemy: On law, rights and proper subjects, *Law, Culture and the Humanities Journal.* Online before print.

2 See also Patrick Hanafin (2011).

3 While the Canadian Supreme Court passed a new judgment in *Carter v Canada* (Attorney General), 2015 SCC 5, [2015] 1 S.C.R. 331 declaring assisted dying legal, we await Parliament's response.

Chapter 3

Inviolable Persons

Sometimes the law will refer to "sanctity of life" and other times it will refer to "quality of life:" in the legal discourse however these two concepts always refer to a life that cannot be penetrated by outside interference; they refer to what legal scholar, Linda McClain (1995: 198), has noted as a body that cannot be violated and must be "impregnable to assault or trespass:" they refer to the concept of inviolability. Inviolability of persons emerges as a concept in assisted dying cases to support the argument that subjects of law cannot be interfered with by outside intrusion. One of the clearest indicators of this concept of inviolability of persons in assisted dying cases is how it is drawn on to invoke a differentiation between what the law calls forms of "killing" or "acts" versus forms of "letting die" or "omissions." England's Anthony Bland's case had set a precedent for this differentiation in which the law referred to Bland's death as a "passive" mode of letting die, in contrast to what the law comparatively dubs "active" forms of killing.

Omissions and Letting Die

We will be reminded that Anthony Bland was the subject of the horrific Hillsborough disaster. At the age of 18 he was trapped in a crush of fans at a football game between Liverpool and Nottingham Forrest. As a result he suffered from broken ribs and punctured lungs, which prevented oxygen from reaching his brain, leaving him in a persistent vegetative state. In his case, judges deliberated over whether or not he could be removed from life sustaining treatment. While the court noted that the state upheld the value of human life and its sanctity, it also noted that in this case the quality of life was of equal importance. The following question was raised:

> What is meant now by "life" in the moral precept which requires respect for the sanctity of human life? If the quality of life of a person such as Anthony Bland is non-existent since he is unaware of anything that happens to him, has he a right to be sustained in that state of living death and are his family and medical attendants under a duty to maintain it?
>
> (*Airedale NHS Trust v Bland* [1993] AC 789: 25)

Later in Bland's case the concept of inviolability emerged, particularly in Lord Hoffman's commentary in which he stated:

> I think, connected with our view that the sanctity of life entails its inviolability by an outsider. Subject to exceptions like self-defence, human life is inviolate even if the person in question has consented to its violation. That is why although suicide is not a crime, assisting someone to commit suicide is. It follows that, even if we think Anthony Bland would have consented, we would not be entitled to end his life by a lethal injection.
>
> (*Airedale NHS Trust v Bland* [1993] AC 789 at 831)

The reference to the inviolability of persons provided a pivotal rationale in defense of letting Bland die and also provided a rationale for maintaining restrictions on other forms of killing. Inviolability of persons allowed the law to articulate a legal fiction of immune persons that closed off the self from that which exists outside of it. This allowed the law to (indeed it demanded that the law) articulate a distinction between what it called "acts" and what it called "omissions;" the former of which was said to interfere with inviolability, and the latter of which could be said to uphold inviolability. For instance, Lord Justice Toulson cited *Bland* in Nicklinson's case of *Nicklinson v MOJ* [2012] EWHC 2381 (Admin) (paragraph 60) noting:

> the judges were acutely aware of the profoundly difficult ethical questions which the case presented. They reached their decision on the legal basis that Anthony Bland's condition was such that the doctors no longer had a legal duty to continue invasive care and treatment, and accordingly the omission to continue such treatment would not be an unlawful omission. They emphasised two things: first, that the law drew a crucial distinction between an omission to maintain treatment and the administration of a lethal drug, however unsatisfactory such a distinction might seem to some

people from an ethical viewpoint; and secondly, that it must be a matter for Parliament to decide whether the law should be changed, taking into account the complex humanitarian, ethical and practical considerations.

Specifically citing Lord Goff at page 865 in *Bland*, Toulston continued (paragraph 60):

> I must however, stress … that the law draws a crucial distinction between cases in which a doctor decides not to provide, or to continue to provide, for his patient treatment or care which could or might prolong his life, and those in which he decides, for example by administering a lethal drug, actively to bring the patient's life to an end. As I have already indicated, the former may be lawful, either because the doctor is giving effect to his patient's wishes by withholding the treatment or care, or even in certain circumstances in which … the patient is incapacitated from stating whether or not he gives his consent. But it is not lawful for a doctor to administer a drug to his patient to bring about his death, even though that course is prompted by a humanitarian desire to end his suffering, however great that suffering may be … So to act is to cross the Rubicon which runs between on the one hand the care of the living patient and the other hand euthanasia—actively causing his death to avoid or to end his suffering.

Again, the precise reason for the enunciation of the concept of inviolability of persons is revealed above as a necessity in order to articulate the differentiation between what the law calls "omissions," which is said to be the practice of "letting" persons die, and what the law calls "acts" which is a technique of the active "killing" of persons and the taking of life. As a precedent, Bland's case has also appeared in the more recent assisted dying appeals that are the focus of this book. The decision in *Bland* continues to be invoked to differentiate between acts of killing and acts (or omissions) of letting die.

Acts and Making Die

Appeals to die that are expressed as "active" are deemed so because they are said to require an active taking of life or killing rather than simply pulling a plug, framed as an omission, as with Bland's case. One of the earliest English legal cases that dealt with an active right to die request was from Dianne Pretty. Pretty's story broke news headlines in 2001. She spoke of the desire for her husband of 25 years, Brian, to be able to help her die, articulated in her two legal cases of *R (Pretty) v Director of Public Prosecutions* [2001] UKHL 61 and *Pretty v The United Kingdom* [2002] ECHR 427, the latter of which took her case to the European Court of Human Rights. Pretty, like Rodriguez and Taylor, was diagnosed in 1999 with motor neurone disease (also known as ALS), which is a progressive neuro-degenerative disease of the central nervous system. Unlike Debbie Purdy, whose appeal came after hers, Pretty did not want her husband to assist her with travel to Dignitas; rather, she was the first in the UK to challenge the existing law regarding the right to have her life ended by another person within the UK.

Pretty had initially appealed to the Director of Public Prosecutions in 2001 to the right to have another person help her die should she reach a point in time when she deemed living with her disease intolerable. When her appeal to the Director of Public Prosecutions in the case of *Pretty v DPP* failed, she took her case to the European Court of Human Rights in *Pretty v UK*. Again, however, her appeal was denied. Pretty's case was one of the first to be denied using *Bland* as *stare decisis* (binding precedent). Following Pretty's case that cited *Bland*, England's Debby Purdy's in *R (Purdy) v Director of Public Prosecutions* [2009] EWCA Civ 92, was also committed to this precedent, revealing at paragraph 38 that:

> while addressing the right of a terminally ill individual to self-determination, and the importance of protecting his or her dignity and quality of life, underlined the prohibition against taking life, "recognising that a terminally ill or dying person's wish to die never constitutes any legal claim to die at the hand of another person ... (and) cannot of itself constitute a legal justification to carry out actions intended to bring about death."

Here we see a direct reference to the impossibility for the law to respond to the prospect of dying "at the hand of another person" and the "actions" that would intentionally kill subjects like Purdy and Pretty. Nicklinson's legal case in 2012 also made this clear. As noted in Chapter 2, Nicklinson's case referenced the notion of dueling and the war-like relation between persons; it also referenced the impossibility for law to respond to compassionate motives for killing because the other, the enemy, could not be trusted. Nicklinson's case used the reference to *Bland* as a defense; it argued that Lord Goff's reference to the Rubicon regarding "the care of the living patient and on the other hand euthanasia—actively causing his death to avoid or to end his suffering" was crossed in other cases (*R (Nicklinson) v Ministry of Justice* [2012] EWHC 2381 (Admin), (2012) MHLO, paragraph 63). On Nicklinson's behalf, dissenting Mr Bowen argued that in the case of *Re A Conjoined Twins* an act was legalized in order to kill one twin, as Chapter 2 outlined. In response to this claim, Toulston noted that these features present in the case of *Re A* were "highly unusual" and were "absent from the present case" (*Nicklinson v MOJ*, 2012, paragraph, 72): it was argued that if a doctor administered Nicklinson a lethal drug "there could be no defence to a charge of murder based on lack of causation, lack of intent or quasi-self-defence" (paragraph 72).

Marie Fleming's case also articulated a similar point. In *Fleming v Ireland & Ors,* Judgment, I EHC 2, 2013, the High Court noted:

> in its judgment, the High Court in this case found that there was a "profound difference" between the law permitting an adult to take their own life on the one had and sanctioning another to assist that person on the other (at paragraph 22). This statement sought to distinguish "active" from "passive" euthanasia perhaps for the purpose of reconciling the Court's decision with the apparent ratio of the Ward judgment, where the withdrawal of life sustaining treatment was authorized.
>
> (Paragraph 21)

The concept of inviolability of persons feeds a legal fiction of the immune person that rationalizes the refusal of active killing with reference to the notion of the assister in death—the outsider who, as Chapter 2 noted, cannot be trusted to offer "help" in dying. Likewise, in *Pretty v DPP* (s.7), Lord Justice Tuckey articulated this distinction in the following way:

> The crucial distinction is between "killing and letting die." English law puts helping someone to take her own life on the wrong side of the line, because, as Hoffman LJ said in *Bland at 831,* "the sanctity of life entails its inviolability by an outsider" (L.831). The question is whether this is in breach of that person's human rights under the Convention.

In Pretty's case, as well as in others, the distinction between killing and letting die is made possible through the concept of the inviolable person, who is a subject that cannot be intruded upon "by an outsider." Ultimately, the rationalization for denying (some forms) of assisted death appears to be intimately linked to the constitution of the person as inviolable that is associated with a defense from outside interference.

Outsiders and Immune Persons

One can note some overlap here with Chapter 2, which examined how law used concepts of enmity and vulnerability to feed a legal fiction of the immune person as he or she who was protected from outside interference. Law has long articulated itself as a mechanism of protection of individual life from what exists "outside." In the contemporary era it is simply that this mechanism of protection has intensified (Campbell, 2011). McClain (1995), for instance, writes that discussions of inviolability emerge in the context of legal discussions regarding privacy, particularly appearing through the articulation of the body as a site of defense from outside interference. She notes that inviolability mostly refers to a freedom from governmental interference or from "outside invasion" (McClain, 1995: 201). Esposito's (2008, 2010, 2013) work on immunization also makes this point: he even more assertively attaches inviolability to personhood arguing that it is "the inviolability of the person [that] has become the guiding light of all democratically inspired social theories" (2012a: 4).

Framing something as an omission rather than as an act allows the law to present the idea that in the case of the former no one is "assisting" with death per se and that the subject who is merely to be "let die" is alone and isolated without any relation to the outsider: the subject is an immune person. Through this concept of inviolability of persons that invokes the notion of the private and secure person who is not subject to intrusion or trespass as the law seems to conjecture, the law is able to feed the fiction of the immune person because it makes it appear that there is no "assistance" in this passive instance of death, but merely an absent presence or a trace of care.

Constructing the Outsider through Medical Techniques

The differentiation between what exists within one's person and what exists outside one's person is a tool to help shape the concept of inviolability of persons that the law requires to feed the fiction of the immune person as he or she who is absolute, whole and impenetrable. Legal decisions will draw on various ideas to differentiate between acts and omissions in order to support this concept of inviolability and the fiction of the immune person that it feeds.

In England, sedation and passive euthanasia were brought together as viable practices of omissions that could be distinguished from "acts" of killing in the case of Bland on the basis of "best interest." Bland's case followed precedent set in *Re J (Minor) (Wardship Medical Treatment)* [1991] 1 Fam. 33 (a case dealing with a prematurely born and brain damaged minor). It argued that a differentiation could be made between omissions (i.e. terminal sedation or a dose of drugs for passive euthanasia patients to help ease pain and passing) and acts (i.e. providing a dose of drugs that would sedate a person in order to actively hasten death to kill the person). The former was defended on the basis of the Doctrine of Double Effect. Lord Donaldson of Lymington MR stated the following at paragraph 46:

> What doctors and the court have to decide is whether, in the best interests of the child patient, a particular decision as to medical treatment should be taken which *as a side effect* will render death more or less likely. This is not a matter of semantics. It is fundamental. Historically this has been framed as a Doctrine of Double Effect. This doctrine states that it is not acceptable to give someone a lethal dose of morphine to kill them; it is only acceptable to give someone a dose of morphine that will ease their pain, even if this may in turn decrease the longevity of their life. The double effect doctrine suggests that the end goal in giving morphine, or what is now referred to as palliative sedation, is not to kill the person but to help them; even though this practice might result in the individual's death, because this was not the principal intention the practice is considered ethical. In this instance the doctrine rationalizes the easing of pain that does not actively set out to kill, or take life. At the other end of the age spectrum, the use of drugs to reduce pain will often be fully justified, notwithstanding that this will hasten the moment of death. What can never be justified is the use of drugs or surgical procedures with the primary purpose of doing so.

Despite law's insistence on the differentiation between omissions and acts, framed and supported by claims of best interest and the Doctrine of Double Effect, scholars and medical ethicists continue to question whether these differentiations can be so clearly made (Billings and Block, 1996; Birnbacher, 2007; Douglas *et al.*, 2008; Miller and Truog, 2011; Shah and Miller, 2010; Sprung *et al.*, 2008). As Billings and Block

(1996), Birnbacher (2007) and more recently Miller and Truong (2011) have suggested, one could just as readily claim that "withdrawing" life support, another intervention currently framed as an omission, is equally as "active" in providing "assistance" in death as giving a person lethal medication to inject into themselves (currently termed assisted suicide), or injecting this medication into them (termed active euthanasia).

Likewise, Birnbacher (2007) argues that legal cases will often draw on the example of palliative/terminal sedation to support the distinction between passive and active forms of legal treatment, claiming that sedative techniques are passive forms of treatment despite the question of whether sedation—as an "act" —notably contradicts this legal difference. Terminal or palliative sedation, which also might overlap in cases of passive euthanasia, involves giving either narcotics (e.g., morphine) or sedatives (e.g., valium), or might also involve barbiturates or other tranquilizing drugs. These drugs are used to sedate the patient until he or she dies, also at the same time as withholding nutrition and hydration (e.g., Orentlicher, 1997). Some have argued that this sedation is not an omission but is better classified as an act, and have referred to this as a 'slow euthanasia" (e.g., Billings and Block, 1996).

Justice Smith in *Carter v Canada* (Attorney General) [2012] BCSC 886 recognized a similar point to Birnbacher's (2007) claim regarding palliative/terminal sedation. Smith noted that questions of palliative sedation have not effectively been given judicial consideration in Canada despite laws often assuming it falls in the category of omissions and passive euthanasia (see *Carter v Canada*, 2012, s. 226). Likewise, in this same case Justice Smith drew on the opinion of ethicist Professor Sumner regarding attempts "to distinguish: acts from omissions; a patient's request for treatment which will hasten death from refusal of a treatment which will prolong life; killing from letting die; and death as an intended outcome from death as an unintended though foreseen outcome" (Paragraph 235). From Sumner's perspective it was impossible "to show that, of the four treatment options (treatment cessation, pain management, terminal sedation and assisted death), assisted death is uniquely ethically impermissible" (Paragraph 235). In the 2015 Supreme Court decision on *Carter v Canada* (Attorney General), 2015 SCC 5, [2015] 1 S.C.R. 331, the court followed Smith's suit and noted that she was right to find that the "preponderance of evidence from ethicists is that there is no ethical distinction between physician assisted death and other end-of-life practices whose outcome is highly likely to be death" (Paragraph 23).

Even in *Bland*, where the distinction was upheld so forcefully, the tenuous grounds upon which the distinctions stood were noted. Lord Goff, cited in *Bland*, noted that the law's distinctions between passive and active forms of killing might be deemed hypocritical, stating: "It is true that the drawing of this distinction may lead to a charge of hypocrisy…But the law does not feel able to authorise euthanasia, even in circumstances such as these; for once euthanasia is recognised as lawful in these circumstances, it is difficult to see any logical basis for excluding it in others" (*Airedale NHS Trust v Bland* [1993] AC 789: 865). An earlier US legal case, *Cruzan v Director, Missouri Department of Health*, 497 U.S., 261, 269. [1990], also recognized that the line drawn between passive and active euthanasia was "unreasonable," comparing it to a ruling that might state that:

> one may not kill oneself by walking into the sea, but may sit on the beach until submerged by the incoming tide; or that one may not intentionally lock oneself into a cold storage locker, but may refrain from coming indoors when the temperature drops below freezing.

Moreover, scholars have claimed even more broadly outside the context of assisted dying that technology and the body intersect in so many areas of life and death that it is impossible to note any kind of medical technique that does not in some way usurp the sharp differentiation between what exists inside or outside the body, what is organic and natural, and what is technologically aided and unnatural (e.g., Esposito, 2008).

If scholars, medical practitioners, ethicists and even the judges themselves note that the differentiation between acts and omissions is tenuous, why does the law insist on upholding it? Why does the law insist on rationalizing practices it deems acceptable via a concept of inviolability of persons that feeds a fiction of immune persons subject to non-interference, and why does the law in turn rationalize practices it deems unacceptable on the basis of the active intrusion these practices would have on the inviolable person? The aim, it seems, is to make a clear distinction between the person and those who exist outside the person: the concept of inviolability of persons, shaped through other ideas and narratives feeding this concept, creates the fiction of the immune person as an absolute sovereign whole.

It is the distinction between the self and outsider that serves to shore up the legal decision to deny acts and allow omissions. Justice Lynn Smith of Gloria Taylor in *Carter v Canada* (Attorney General) [2012]

BCSC 886 clearly made this point when she also called on Sumner's distinction between the laws on suicide and laws on assisted suicide, that overlaps with the commentary of Lord Goff in *Bland* and Judge Nicholas Kearns in *Fleming*. Sumner stated: "While suicide remains within personal boundaries (leaving aside spillover effects on others), assistance crosses those boundaries: it is action not by a person on herself but by one person upon another" (Paragraph 237).

This reading of legal appeals to assisted death seems to comply with the commentary of other scholars who have called attention to the "bounded individual" who appears in law: this is the private, secured and "bordered" person (Naffine, 2009; Nedelsky, 2012). This also corresponds to what Goffman called the "territories of the self." From Nedelsky's (1990: 168–169) perspective, the boundary metaphor invoked in law:

> invites us to imagine that the self to be protected is in some critical sense insular, and that what is most important to the preservation of such a self is drawing boundaries around it that will protect it from invasion (or at least that is the most crucial thing the law can do).

Nedelsky here appears to also note the very way that the concept of inviolability feeds the legal fiction of the immune person: the bounded person is constituted as a fiction that fulfills the function of immunization that divides subjects from one another. As noted previously, Campbell (2011) suggests that this bordered self does not only appear through liberalism, as Esposito himself recognizes, but also becomes increasingly prevalent in the neoliberal era. For Campbell, neoliberalism with its proliferation and intensification of privacy and self-interestedness has the impact of increasing these defensive borders of the self. A neoliberal political rationality thrives off, and indeed proliferates, the legal fiction of immune persons in its efforts to complete its goal: an immune society; a totality of immune persons who are reciprocally dissociated from one another.

Norms of Life, Personalization and the Immune Society

If neoliberalism requires that subjects be immunized from one another as individual units within a larger totality, surely one could argue that taking Bland's life actively could have been legitimated within this larger totalizing logic. Bland's legal case constructed him as absolutely dependent on life support machines and on others to allow him to live.

Likewise, I have already noted that appellants who seek assisted death are also framed as burdens on the state and on others. Their deaths might be revered from the vantage of a neoliberal ethos. So, why does the law use the concept of inviolability to appear to protect these lives if it might be more helpful for the rationality to allow them to be killed?

In defense of this claim one might point to a number of historical moments in which subjects have been depersonalized and the law has been able to rationalize this without the need of a personalizing safeguard. One could note for instance that under other historical practices, which have operated with similar immunizing mechanisms that attempt to govern by individualizing and totalizing subjects, law has managed to retain itself and its fiction of immune persons by way of mere depersonalization of other subjects. For example, one could refer to the practices of Nazi Germany. Esposito (2008) argues that German law rationalized "active killing" through an absolute depersonalization of subjects such that those who were being killed were considered "already dead." The German subjects who were killed were not enunciated within the fiction of the immune person: they were not immune; instead they threatened the immune society, the totality of immune subjects. The law simply depersonalized them such that they fell outside the prospect of immunity per se. Killing the "already dead" was considered of immunitary benefit for those subjects who were considered alive and immune persons under law.

Given this previous immune logic that could apparently rationalize such death, why did the law not in this instance also merely claim that Bland was "already dead" (i.e. as a ventilated corpse) such that it may have had no need to differentiate between passive and active killing? If Bland was conceived as dead, any action upon him could have been rationalized as passive—as a mere continuation of and finalization of his death. Conversely, one might also question why the law did not, for instance, articulate Bland's death on the basis of a defense of society like the law did with the self-defense of the person in the case of *Re A (Children) (Conjoined Twins Surgical Separation)*. Why instead did the law allow the concept of inviolability of persons to feed the legal fiction of the immune person in the case of Bland?

Protecting Each and All: The Fiction of the Immune Society

That the law did not rationalize Bland's death this way, but rather conferred upon him some notion of legal personhood, is arguably telling; it also helps explain why a consideration of the contemporary political rationality and climate is important. Arguably it is telling of the close association between the two legal fictions emergent in assisted dying laws: the immune society requires the protection of each and of all. It is attached to a larger totalizing rationality that neoliberalism expresses which claims that "all" life is protected, particularly in the aftermath of other atrocities like Nazi Germany that have compelled contemporary liberal democracies to expand universal human rights in order to protect us from this prospect.

Esposito (2008, 2012a, 2012b, 2013) himself has noted the increased mechanisms of immunization that have arisen post Nazi Germany; since then personhood appears to be granted upon all subjects in the view that it was a lack of personhood (and its associated rights) that led to Nazi atrocities. The law appears to prohibit the prospect of depersonalization and instead invokes the concept of inviolability to actively claim equality for persons—such as with the Universal Declaration of Human Rights; this allows the law to claim that it is not operating within the same semantics of depersonalization (Esposito, 2012a). The law as a discourse and technology of a neoliberal governance rationality must at least appear to be protecting persons, even if at the heart of this personalization is a simultaneous depersonalization and a differentiation being accorded on the basis of an ascribed quality of life that is made with the same kind of decisions about whose life has value and whose does not. Law must at least appear to protect persons and confer personhood upon each and every subject; it must at least generate the fiction of the immune person within the immune society. It has done so by bringing all subjects under law as immune persons through a universal declaration of rights that overtly articulates the category of personhood for each and all and claims not to differentiate between subjects and their life's quality, despite it being precisely this category of personhood itself that makes such differentiation possible (Esposito, 2012a; Naffine, 2009). This alleged universalization of immune person is part of the totalization logic of neoliberalism that has also allowed an even deeper division between subjects.

This does not mean that neoliberalism actually protects more subjects than ever before; rather, it means to suggest that neoliberalism has had to find other ways to allow subjects to die in compliance with the neoliberal immune community without seeming, by way of appearance, to be as destructive as Nazism. Indeed Esposito notes this when he claims that even though personhood has apparently been granted to all subjects by way of universal human rights and so on, by virtue of its immunizing particularity—that is, since being immune is a privilege—it would be impossible to sustain a society of fully immune persons who are absolutely reciprocally dissociated from one another.

Subtle Depersonalizations

Recalling *Bland*, one might indicate that he was not depersonalized per se, but rather his depersonalization was less overt. The law operating as a norm makes different, less apparent instances of depersonalization possible. Arguably this is the precise issue that Peter Singer (1994) misses in his own analysis. Singer and others like him (e.g., Huxtable, 2002) considers liberal politics in a vacuum: he does not try to bring the subject in line with broader governance objectives of the state, but rather takes legal decisions at face value and in the context of liberalism reads the decision in *Bland* as a mere acceptance of the values of liberal individualism without considering how liberal individualism is bound to a larger governmental rationality. One could note for example that law has to operate more as a norm in the present context given the pervasiveness of universal human rights. In the contemporary neoliberal governmental context, which arguably is one that at least in appearance has alleged to have rolled back the intrusion of the state at the same time as having increased security around persons, the constitution of inviolable personhood in legal cases is necessary; it operates in a similar way to the concept of freedom that Rose (1999) has commented on: in much the same way that our freedom is given to us so that we can be free in ways that are shaped by governance mechanisms, so too is our inviolable personhood given to us at least nominally by way of law to appear to protect subjects even if a larger political rationality is shaping "who counts" as a subject in different kinds of ways (Esposito, 2012a, 2013).

A number of socio-legal scholars have recently pointed to the operation of legal personhood as a mechanism that law uses to both target its object and rationalize its legal decision (e.g., Esposito, 2012a, 2012b, 2013; Naffine, 2009; Nedelsky, 1990, 2012; Pavlich, 2012a, 2012b, 2013). Various scholars have argued that legal processes play a key role in constituting different kinds of subjects (Hardes *et al.* 2014; Lacey, 2001a, 2001b, 2007; Naffine, 2003; Pavlich, 2007, 2009, 2013). This means to suggest that persons are the targets of law: law relies on categories of persons in order to fix its target. Law's assumptions about persons often performatively configure the subject as a particular kind of person. As Pavlich (2013: 3) convincingly writes "discursive enunciations of persons enable ... law to settle its gaze differently on different categories of persons." This is so because law is not a neutral or objective institution but rather law operates as a discourse and technology of a particular rationality of governance. For example, Pavlich argued in the context of his work on criminal law at the Cape Colony that the construction of various categories of personhood permitted law to operate in accordance with a political rationality that governed through the appearance of a sovereign regime of power. This allowed the law to ascribe different punishments on the basis of differentiations between persons.

This treatment of persons and personhood's enunciative function is a key point that Esposito (2012a, 2012b, 2013) has also raised; he has claimed that law operates through a continual personalization and depersonalization by way of the constitution of legal categories of person: no one is a person by nature, but only by way of law:

> What Roman law achieves with such incomparable categorical imagination is not only the distinction among persons, semipersons, and nonpersons but also elaborations of intermediate situations, zones of indistinction, and exceptions that regulate the movement, or oscillation, from one status to another.
>
> (Esposito, 2013: 115)

Personalization and depersonalization is strategic, notes Esposito. Personhood allows the generation of the legal fiction of the immune person because it allows law to settle its gaze on an object and immunize it.

Foucault was very aware of the very juridico-medical apparatus at play, writing: "it [medicine] infiltrates law, it plugs into it, it makes it work. A sort of juridico-medical complex is presently being constituted which is the major form of power" (1996b: 197). He made it clear that legal fictions such as the immune person are constituted through the complex interaction between science, medicine, politics and law. Legal judgments that legitimate decisions through the constitution of concepts like inviolability of persons that sustain a differentiation between acts and omissions tend to obscure the role of politics and power in this determination of what life "counts" and what life does not: the legal judgment becomes but a moral trace—erasing the decision and immunizing the decider.

In short, the concept of inviolability of persons feeds the legal fiction of the universal immune person within an immune totality: this detracts from the more subtle ways that subjects are depersonalized. For example, although the legal cases did note that Bland's life was futile, the case was careful not to use this as the overriding rationality for allowing him to die: rather, it emphasized how allowing him to die (or we might argue, killing him) was not a decision on the value of his life per se, but rather confirmed the value of all life that requires legal protection. Simply because the act of killing was legitimated on the basis of non-interference does not mean that a value was not attached to the life being taken; rather, it means that the value accorded to the life was made through less overt means in accordance with a political rationality that claims to protect all life equally, while finding other ways to depersonalize, in this instance through what was claimed to be an omission and a "letting die."

The opening pages of the book suggested that the law operates more as a norm: in this case, one can note that personhood was necessarily conferred upon Bland overtly for the sake of being able to differentiate between an acceptable legal practice and an unacceptable one; the acceptable practice (passive killing) could be rationalized by suggesting that it did not "violate" or intrude upon the person per se because the immune person could technically remain intact, whilst the unacceptable act (active killing) could not in this instance be rationalized without a violation of the immune person himself or herself.

Protecting (Some) Outsiders: Immunizing Medical Practitioners

The personalization of Bland through the concept of inviolability was also important for another reason. It legitimated the killing of Bland through an act that would comport with a logic of non-interference: the personalization of Bland rationalized the pulling of the plug as simply an omission that did not interfere with his "inviolable person." We will be reminded that in *Bland*, Lord Browne-Wilkinson had discussed the potential for prosecution of physicians in terms of murder on the basis of *mens rea* and *actus reus*. While he claimed that *mens rea* (i.e. guilty mind) would apply in the case of Bland, he noted that the *actus reus* (guilty act) would not be found in withdrawing treatment because it was an act of omission versus a positive act:

> In my judgment, essentially what is being done is to omit to feed or to ventilate: the removal of the nasogastric tube or the switching off of a ventilator are merely incidents of that omission: see Glanville Williams, *Textbook of Criminal Law*, 2nd ed. (1983), p. 282, Skegg p. 169 et seq.
>
> (*Airedale NHS Trust v Bland* [1993] AC 789: 29)

Further, at page 29, he states:

> The removal of the tube by itself does not cause the death since by itself it did not sustain life. Therefore even if, contrary to my view, the removal of the tube is to be classified as a positive act, it would not constitute the actus reus of murder since such positive act would not be the cause of death.

In short, he claimed that the physician did not owe a positive duty of care. One opposing claim, however, was that the doctors had a positive duty to provide care for Bland because they had initiated his care. However, because competent persons could refuse medical treatment, granting an omission in some cases of refusal was deemed acceptable.

While Bland did not have the capacity to refuse treatment, a lacuna in the law meant that no precedent was set before him. One proposal was to fill this space with the notion of necessity and best interests. The case drew on *Re F (Mental Patient: Sterilisation)* [1990] 2 A.C.1 in support. *Re F* had placed necessity as a rationale for intervening with the person when mentally incompetent. This was only made in terms of best interests of the patient:

> further continuance of an intrusive life support system is not in the best interests of the patient, he can no longer lawfully continue that life support system: to do so would constitute the crime of battery and the tort of trespass to the person. Therefore he cannot be in breach of any duty to maintain the patient's life. Therefore he is not guilty of murder by omission.
>
> (*Airedale NHS Trust v Bland*, paragraph 29)

Two things were framed here that are interesting for the present discussion. First, as already noted, Bland's inviolable, and immune, personhood was necessary to frame the difference between acts and omissions and rationalize the taking of his life by the latter, in a sense that preserved him as a private individual protected from interference. Second, and at the same time as preserving Bland as a private individual, it also preserved the immunity of the person taking his life, ensuring this person was also not subject to legal stricture. On this latter note, the case framed the continuation of medical care as that which would constitute battery and trespass. Such trespass would be akin to an interference with the private person, which would be said to actively contradict the legal fiction of the immune person and therefore also contradict a political rationality of neoliberalism that this legal fiction perpetuates which places increased emphasis on the importance of privacy and non-interference. Constituting Bland as a person was necessary in order to claim that keeping him alive would be deemed battery and assault on his inviolable person, and that letting him die would not constitute such an assault, nor would it interfere with the concept of inviolability feeding the fiction of Bland as an immune person. The case claimed that protecting Bland's body from inhumane medical treatment was in his best interest, which relied on him being a person to have such an interest: it was worse to keep him alive than "allow" him to die.

In framing Bland's death this way, and in removing the trace of assistance by way of this differentiation between act and omission, the law enunciated a second level of immunization that claimed to protect not only the subject of assisted death (either it is an acceptable death like Bland's or it is protecting subjects—those active appellants—from an unacceptable death and outside interference) but also to protect those who would be complicit in taking life (or letting die as we have been told). Legitimating omissions on the basis that this does not actively intervene with the inviolable, immune person, also immunizes the practitioner who "pulls the plug." By bringing the process of omission into the legal fiction of immune personhood, the withdrawal of care continues to be conceived of as a personalizing act, complicit with neoliberalism's legal fictions of the immune person and immune society and the ethos of non-interference. The immune person, or medical practitioner, who took Bland's life was not constituted as a murderer because he or she were not said to have actively killed Bland or interfered with his inviolable, immune person. Rather, by framing the omission as non-interference it could be articulated that the taking of his life occurred by way of respect for his proper person; this would be entirely consistent with a neoliberal political rationality that preserves immunized subjects who are held in relations of reciprocal non-interference through governmental technologies such as law. This neoliberal ethos of non-interference, enunciated through concept of inviolability of persons that feeds the legal fictions of immune persons and immune society, is evident in an increased emphasis on the individual subject of rights who is protected from the state and any other outside interference including that of medical professionals (Lavi, 2008), and might be said to absolutely be reflected within these legal cases and their rationalization through the concept of inviolability.

Where it has been noted that the problem with assisted suicide is that it crosses the boundaries of the inviolable person and threatens the fiction of the immune person, it can also be noted how this rationale impacts medical professionals. Drawing on Glanville Williams (1983), Lord Goff stated in *Bland* that what "the doctor does when he switches off a life support machine 'is in substance not an act but an omission to struggle', and that 'the omission is not a breach of duty by the doctor because he is not obliged to continue in a hopeless case'."

Miller and Truong (2011) suggest that the distinction between acts and omissions is a necessary fiction constituted through law and medicine to keep the medical profession away from an association with death and killing. Bringing their argument back in line with this book that suggests the concept of inviolability is necessary to feed the fiction of the immune person, that allows the differentiation between acts and omissions, one could argue that the concept of inviolability feeds the fiction of the doctor as an immune person. It is not simply that the fiction immunizes the subject of assisted death (e.g., Bland, and so on) but that it also feeds the fiction of he or she who can assist in this death via an omission. Even if the doctor's assistance constitutes an "act," it makes this act acceptable by way of the concept of inviolability that feeds an image of a doctor performing an acceptable act (omission) on an immune person, in order to maintain themselves also as good immune persons who do not interfere with others. This is a necessary part of the immune process, and the legal decision to deny assisted dying on the basis of a concept of inviolability is useful because it protects the medical professional from appearing to violate a universal immunity granted to each and every person. As Miller and Truong (2011) argue, the law and medicine have a stake in immunizing the medical profession from acts that would be seen to contradict with their practice based on values of life and care.

Indeed in *Rodriguez* this was highlighted as a possible reason to refuse assisted dying: it would impose an unfair obligation on medical professionals to take life that would be inconsistent with the tenets of their practice. At paragraph 120, Sopinka stated:

> Since much of the medical profession is opposed to being involved in assisting suicide because it is antithetical to their role as healers of the sick, many doctors will refuse to assist, leaving open the potential for the growth of a macabre specialty in this area reminiscent of Dr. Kervorkian and his suicide machine.

From Miller and Truong's (2011) perspective, the law creates fictions regarding a difference between acts and omissions not only to allow some acts and deny others, but also to protect medical professionals from the possibility of this type of association with death. It might be argued, for instance, that a dissociation between medicine and death is important to preserve the medical profession's alleged responsibility toward maintaining life, and also might be necessary to preserve fiduciary relationships with patients. Bioethicist Brendan Leier (2013) has even claimed that to preserve such a relationship, whilst euthanasia might itself become a legal prospect, the act of killing in euthanasia ought to be passed over to the military, a profession engaged with taking life. This is in contrast to some of the suggestions put forward by Justice Lynn Smith in *Carter v Canada* (2012) that concluded that changes in the physician–patient relationship following legalization may not actually harm the relationship between the patient and the doctor but rather "could prove to be neutral or for the good" (Paragraph 746). A logic of closure, protection and "immunization" of the doctor from the act of taking the life of the patient is not the only inevitable option as it is often presented.

Medicine, Immunity and Death

While the separation between medicine and death might appear "neat" and "clear-cut," it seems that one could also note a lineage of medicine that has been associated quite visibly with death; to attempt to obscure this association presents yet another fiction that ignores a wealth of historical instances in which death and medicine have been closely associated (e.g., Agamben, 1998; Frank, 1976; Marshall, 1995).[1] For Agamben (1998) this association between medicine and death was especially prevalent—indeed, it culminated—in Nazi Germany whereby medical practitioners themselves suggested Nazism's euthanizing techniques and played a key role in administering them through policies such as T4, which euthanized persons with disabilities and others deemed "degenerate." Esposito (2008: 113) also writes of this direct involvement of physicians in the atrocities of Nazi Germany, whereby they participated in "all of the phases of mass homicide ... No step in the production of death escaped medical verification." Recalling the legal disposition of Victor Brack who was head of the Reich's Euthanasia Department, Esposito (2008: 113) further posits that only physicians "had the right to inject phenol into the heart of victims or to open the gas valve." Indeed, this is one of the strongest critiques one could level at scholars such as Singer (1994) and Huxtable (2002) who claim from a liberal vantage to be in favor of assisted death. Singer, for instance, has forcefully argued that society and law should hand over decisions regarding a person's quality of life and the prospect of assisted death to medical professionals. He claims that hopeless cases such as Bland should be terminated because these subjects are not proper persons: Bland has been sufficiently depersonalized, lacks a quality of life and physicians should be able to determine when to take such an unqualified life without having to suffer a threat of punishment. Problematically, however, Singer's analysis, like others (e.g., Huxtable, 2002), divorces medical decisions over life from the political rationality underpinning the medical decision. In doing so he ascribes a neutrality to medicine that fails to note its role in what Foucault (1996) calls a juridico-medical complex: Singer fails to pay attention to an entire history that links medicine and politics and fails to note how the decision of what life is deemed good and of value and what life is not is a biojuridical one, as Swiffen (2011) and Amendola (2012) have recognized, based on a history of legal fictions that are tied to larger schemes and relations of power and knowledge.

As Esposito and others have cautioned, the atrocities in Nazi Germany did not arise because of an absence of medical ethics, but rather precisely because of its presence: that is, because of a presence "of a medical ethics perverted into its opposite" (Esposito, 2008: 115). Given the controversy that surrounded Nazi Germany and the involvement of medical professionals in fulfilling the promises of the pure Nazi state (Esposito, 2008), it is no stretch of the imagination to consider the ways that law might try to immunize medical practitioners by bringing some acts within legal stricture in a way that does not allege to comport with eugenicist ideas about the appellant's quality of life (i.e. as unqualified), but that reveals the political rationality of governance operating through law as a norm: legal decisions might be rationalized on the basis that they feed the legal fictions of the immune person in order to legitimate more subtle dividing mechanisms, such as the differentiation between acts and omissions, and the differentiation noted earlier regarding positive obligations to provide care versus the prospect of refusal of treatment. Differentiating between acts and omissions without considering how the distinction is made possible only by reference to a concept of inviolability that feeds a legal fiction of the immune person is dangerous: it tries to sidestep the slippery slope arguments that lead to an analogy drawn between end of life terminations like Bland and active killings like those of Nazi Germany.

It is thus important to ask the following: if assisted dying were to be legalized, how would the act of assistance in death be rationalized in this legal discussion? Would or could the act of killing be rationalized via non-interference in a similar way that "passive" euthanasia cases have been rationalized? Moreover, if this were the case, in what ways might this give some persons the outcome they hope (e.g., the right to die), yet through a legal process that is potentially harmful and complicit with the political rationality of neoliberalism that remains based on a logic of division and immunization and that feeds the same legal fictions of immune persons and immune society? As noted in Chapter 2, for instance, Nicklinson's articulation of "not being vulnerable" had a tendency to share the same logic and rationality that did not undo the legal fiction of the immune person and immune society but instead shored it up. How could an affirmative politics be imagined that does not rationalize legal decisions based on norms of life that either get articulated as overt depersonalizations (e.g., in Nazi Germany), or get articulated as overt instances of personalization in which the mechanisms of depersonalization are at work in seemingly more subtle yet pervasive ways (e.g., in the contemporary climate where depersonalization is rationalized through the concept of inviolability of persons that gives the appearance of personhood while concealing the distinction between persons through a different distinction between acts and omissions)?

Conclusion

As this chapter has argued, the law in the contemporary moment appears to generate legal fictions in order to shore up of the limits of human relationality: it does so by allowing some subjects (e.g., medical personnel) to take life in ways that are rationalized through a concept of the inviolability of persons that sustains a fiction of the immune person and the immune society framed as non-interference that is fitting with the larger neoliberal rationality. The legal fiction of the immune person and immune society underscored by the concept of the inviolability of persons allows medical practitioners to "let" some subjects die while not being seen to kill others: it (a) immunizes medical practitioners from being seen as a handmaiden of the state; and (b) divorces the question of assisted dying from a larger question about the ways that life is given value much akin to a eugenic, Nazi logic. Indeed, this seems to echo what Esposito (2012a, 2012b) had suggested with regard to the operation of personhood and its articulations of human rights and the protection of persons. Where personhood is often deemed to be an ethic that ought to be expanded to all persons, what we see here is the very way that it is not a lack of personhood that is the problem, but the very expansion of personhood. The concept of inviolability is thus necessary in the contemporary moment in shoring up acceptable limits of human relationships.

This chapter has argued that the concept of inviolability of persons emerges as a central element of the legal rationalization of the denial of assisted dying. It feeds legal fictions of the immune person and immune society that in turn rationalizes a legal distinction between acts and omissions, even though these distinctions are themselves made on the basis of a set of norms regarding life that reflect a broader neoliberal political rationality. Thus the division between acts and omissions is necessary to do three key things. First, it secures a legal fiction of an immune person that is ultimately expressive of a neoliberal idea of a bordered subject who cannot be interfered with. Second, it legitimates the death of some subjects who would otherwise be regarded as a burden by virtue of maintaining their personhood to negate a slippery slope accusation and to also protect and immunize medical personnel from these accusations. Third, it legitimates and brings into legal stricture the appropriateness of some persons (medical practitioners) performing acts of killing that comport with acceptable practices that are acceptable precisely because they also comport with neoliberal values of non interference (omission). To conclude, the distinction between acts (acts and omissions) that occurs through a fiction of immune persons maintained through the concept of inviolability is an enunciation of a neoliberal political rationality that divides subjects from one another.

Although we are aware that the distinction of acts (i.e. act versus omission) is made possible through the concept of inviolability and although we are also aware that the legal fiction of the immune person is not neutral or innocent but rather is attached to norms of life perpetuated through a rationality of governance (in this case neoliberal) (Dayan, 2011), it does not mean to suggest that the law will not find a way to legitimate practices of what it has thus far called "active" assisted death. The caution here is to continue to analyze the reasons the law provides for denying assisted dying and also to analyze what concepts emerge (like inviolability) to feed legal fictions that enunciate the rationality; it is then that one must deconstruct these decisions on the basis of the assumptions law makes. In all accounts, a necessary consideration is how law creates fictions that reflect a neoliberal political rationality; how in doing so these fictions shore up limits of human relationships; and what truths law claims to present (i.e. inviolable persons) in order to legitimate this very shoring up and constitution of the fictions of the immune person and immune society.

Finally, noting the centrality of inviolability of persons in this chapter also adds to broader scholarly discussion that has thus far focused on the sanctity of life and quality of life in Bland's case. Scholars such as Singer (1994) and Huxtable (2002) have famously asserted that Bland's case represented a turning point in English law: *Bland* represented a shift from archaic notions of life's sanctity toward more liberal leanings in law. Analyzing legal cases in relation to wider power-knowledge relations instead reveals that it is the concept of inviolability of persons that connects both passive and active cases; by showing how both sets of cases are connected with the consistent concept of inviolability of persons that feeds a legal fiction of the immune person and immune society operating on the basis of an illusion of a proper, bordered subject, the chapter also challenges these former theses held by Singer and Huxtable.

Following discussions in this chapter, the next chapter also considers how concepts emerging in right to die legal appeals emphasize the protection of something that appears as a unified whole. This unified whole discussed in the Chapter 4, analogous in some ways to the concept of inviolability presented here in Chapter 3, is the notion of the inviolability of society itself: the following chapter focuses more fully on the legal fiction of the immune society as it is fed through the concept of security.

Note

1 Despite Agamben's contention that this integration of medicine and law is a relatively modern issue that reached its apex when physicians administered death on behalf of the Nazi state, one might note that such medical involvement with law and state affairs regarding death has occurred for centuries. The role of medicine in disseminating death on the part of the state, and making use of state-killed subjects for medical advancement, has a long and callous history. By way of example, we can note the integration of medicine, death, and state law in England, prior to the 1800s (Frank, 1976; Marshall, 1995). For instance, the use of cadavers for medical purposes was also a key instance of the juridico-medical apparatus that Foucault notes in The Birth of the Clinic, which cultivated a normalizing society through medicine. However, for Singer and others who do not consider such social histories, it seems that medicine remains nonpartisan. Politics has no bearing—nor should it—on the determination of the quality of one's life and the medical decisions made on this basis; this perspective is upheld regardless of the historical trajectory within which one can speculate that medical decisions and actions might not prove completely neutral or innocent.

Chapter 4

Security of Persons and of Society

In different ways the previous two chapters have emphasized a common point: both have articulated simultaneous universalizing and particularizing mechanisms of law. Chapter 2 argued that the legal cases drew on concepts of vulnerability and enmity to create the legal fictions of the immune person (particularizing) and the immune society (universalizing). Enmity and vulnerability were articulated as concepts because they allowed the law to fix subjects according to a negative anthropology of humanity that decided in advance that each subject was an immanent enemy of each other subject. The concepts of enmity and vulnerability enabled law to rationalize its protection of each individual person (immune person) while continuing to protect and divide said persons from one another (immune society). Similarly, Chapter 3 argued that legal cases articulated the concept of the inviolable person to generate a legal fiction of the immune person who could not be interfered with from outsiders, also as part of a larger immune society. The concept of the inviolability of persons fed the legal fiction of the immune person that allowed the law to create distinctions between "acts" and "omissions" in assisted dying cases. Where an act was said to interfere with the inviolable person and therefore did not sustain the legal fiction of the immune person, an omission was said to comply with the legal fiction because it did not penetrate the inviolable body of the subject. Passive euthanasia, for instance, was accepted because law framed it as a withdrawal of care and an omission, as opposed to an act of "trespassing" or "intervening" with the person. This allowed the law to refuse the prospect of other forms of assisted death that were not alleged to comport with the legal fiction of the immune person and would otherwise threaten that fiction. In tandem, these chapters showed how legal fictions of the immune person and immune society were complicit with, and enunciated, a neoliberal political rationality that necessarily emphasizes relations of non-interference between subjects who are held in common only by virtue of their reciprocal dissociation from one another.

Along similar lines, this chapter focuses on universalizing and particularizing aspects of law. It focuses specifically on the concept of security as it appears in legal cases on assisted dying in order to give further content to legal fictions of immune persons and immune society, complicit with a neoliberal political rationality. The chapter argues that the concept of security emerges in the legal cases in two ways that appear contradictory: the first is the concept of the secure society and the second is the concept of the secure person. The latter is said to threaten the former: security of persons seeks the defense of individual rights within law; security of society claims that these rights can be overturned (or effectively discounted) if these rights are said to threaten or intervene with a justice in the name of the good of the whole population. The chapter argues that in order to deny assisted dying cases, the former concept of the secure society must feed a legal fiction of the immune society that outweighs and overrides (or that can effectively fold within itself) the concept of the secure person that feeds the fiction of the immune person without threatening this latter fiction. Law does so by appearing to present a balance of interests, whilst at the same time articulating the security of persons as "positive obligations" and "liberty interests," both of which are viewed as threatening to the good immune society of immune persons.

Security of Persons and of Society

In the two major Canadian assisted dying cases of Sue Rodriguez and Gloria Taylor the appellants appealed to section 7 of the Charter of Rights and Freedoms, specifically, the "security of the person." Section 7 encompassed the following elements:

> Security of the person in s. 7 encompasses notions of personal autonomy (at least with respect to the right to make choices concerning one's own body), control over one's physical and psychological integrity which is free from state interference, and basic human dignity.
>
> (*Rodriguez v British Columbia* (Attorney General) [1993] 3 S.C.R. 519, case introduction)

Those dissenting in Rodriguez's case argued that the prohibition of assisted dying under section 241(b) of the Canadian Criminal Code, which states that "Every one who ... aids or abets a person to commit suicide, whether suicide ensues or not, is guilty of an indictable offence and liable to imprisonment for a term not exceeding fourteen years" was a violation of this right to personal security. The case continued:

> The prohibition in s. 241(b), which is a sufficient interaction with the justice system to engage the provisions of s. 7, deprives the appellant of autonomy over her person and causes her physical pain and psychological stress in a manner which impinges on the security of her person.
>
> (*Rodriguez v B.C.*, 1993, case introduction)

Gloria Taylor's case in *Carter v Canada* (Attorney General) [2012] BCSC 886 also established similar grounds for an argument noting that the provisions on assisted dying "deprived the plaintiffs of their rights to life, liberty and security of the person" (Section 13, paragraph 1).

In response, the law invoked the principle of "fundamental justice." Universalizing, fundamental principles of justice, simply referred to as "fundamental justice," are articulated within the 1982 Canadian Constitution in Section 7 of the Canadian Charter of Rights and Freedoms. Though recognized to be a controversial legal principle, as Justice Lynn Smith argued in her judgment of the assisted dying appeal of Gloria Taylor (*Carter v Canada*, 2012), fundamental justice is typically invoked in common law as a legal principle that grants the ability for the law to constitutionally deny individual legal rights if the upholding of these individual rights would be seen to breach fundamental justice. In particular, fundamental justice is referred to in relation to the concept of the security of society as opposed to the security of the individual person. As the Canadian Charter reads in Section 7 of "Life, liberty and security of person:" "Everyone has the right to life, liberty and security of the person and the right not to be deprived thereof except in accordance with the principles of fundamental justice." In general, the legal deferral to fundamental justice legitimates the law's breach of individuals' rights if it considers such a breach (or better, articulates such a breach) in the interests of ensuring that society is protected (e.g., Plaxton, 2008).[1]

Rodriguez and Taylor's assisted dying appeals called on the principle of fundamental justice to determine whether in the case of assisted dying the principle of fundamental justice could outweigh the legal claim to security of persons. Rodriguez and Taylor's cases both argued that the security of the person was entirely consistent with fundamental justice rather than being a principle that opposed it. The dissenting

Justice McLachlin in *Rodriguez* argued that the right to human dignity (or security of persons as it had earlier been framed) was itself a principle of fundamental justice because it must apply to everyone as part of law's role to protect persons. The law had a *positive obligation* to protect the security of the person, and Rodriguez and Taylor both considered the right to an assisted death to be one example of the duty of law to take positive steps to secure this right.

In general the court in Rodriguez's case agreed that personal security was at stake, and Justice Sopinka conceded that the appellant's security interests were engaged. He noted for instance at paragraph 137 that the prohibition in s. 241(b) of the Canadian Criminal Code deprived Rodriguez of "autonomy over her person" and in causing her pain and psychological stress did impinge on the security of her person. However, despite this recognition, Sopinka was undecided on whether the deprivation of security of the person was "in accordance with the principles of fundamental justice" (Paragraph 122). He argued that a consensus of reasonable people underscored fundamental justice: in Rodriguez's case the majority observed that human life must be respected and that the courts should not undermine institutions that insured it (*Rodriguez v B.C.* [1993], paragraph 16, 17; *Carter v Canada* [2012], paragraph 928). Essentially, for Sopinka, determining whether interference with personal security was unjustifiable before allowing assisted death was still important.

From Sopinka's perspective the protection of society demanded adherence to principles of fundamental justice. If assisted dying were legalized, society would be left vulnerable. He thus denied Rodriguez's appeal and stated emphatically:

> The principles of fundamental justice are concerned not only with the interest of the person who claims his liberty [p. 594] has been limited, but with the protection of society. Fundamental justice requires that a fair balance be struck between these interests, both substantively and procedurally.
>
> (*Rodriguez v B.C.* [1993], paragraph 146)

According to Sopinka, Rodriguez's interest in securing her person could not be complicit with fundamental justice because the principle of securing the person would render fundamental justice void. The purpose of fundamental justice, he argued, was to balance the legal rights of individuals to legal protection with the law's duty to protect society as a whole and ensure that these individual rights could be maintained. In the case of assisted dying, the demands of the individual would breach law's role as a mechanism of the protection of life and would invariably open up the prospect of killing (which he claimed was "intrinsically morally and legally wrong"). This possibility of killing posed too grave a threat to those the law intended to protect: the vulnerable (see paragraph 162). In this sense the law rationalized the need to breach the individual right and security of persons on the basis of fundamental justice and security of society because the protection of society outweighed this right: in this case, the law used the principle of fundamental justice in accordance with the concept of security of society to feed the legal fiction of an immune society that was a necessary totality.

Almost 20 years later, Taylor's ruling heard a similar discussion under Justice Lynn Smith regarding this same tension between the individual's security of her person versus the principles of fundamental justice and the security of society. Yet Smith's decision, unlike Sopinka's, claimed that principles of fundamental justice could never outweigh the individual's security interests; instead, Smith claimed fundamental justice was overbroad and grossly disproportionate. One could not place, as with *Rodriguez*, an absolute value on life or insist that all persons were vulnerable. By the end of her extensive case comprised of 1417 paragraphs and 116 affidavits, and a cross examination of 18 witnesses all of which filled 36 binders, Smith declared Taylor a constitutional exemption: this permitted Taylor a physician-assisted suicide within the period of one year whilst the tenets of the law on assisted dying were further considered.

Later, however, in an appeal from the Attorney General (supported by a number of interest groups) in *Carter v Canada* (Attorney General) [2013[BCCA 435, the 2012 ruling was overturned. Justice Smith in *Carter v Canada* [2012] BCSC 886 had claimed that elements of Taylor's case were "new:" the question of assisted dying had not been sufficiently dealt with in Rodriguez's case. Framing elements of Taylor's case as new meant that Smith could legally reopen the debate on assisted dying laws within her court without being bound by *stare decisis* (binding precedent) to apply *Rodriguez*. However, in the Attorney General's appeal, the majority (per Newbury and Saunders JJ.A.) disagreed with Smith and argued that Smith—who was from a lower court—was indeed bound by *stare decisis* to apply *Rodriguez*. While Chief Justice Finch noted in a dissenting opinion that the facts of Taylor's case could be upheld, Justices Newbury and Saunders stated that the decision held in *Rodrgiuez* set a precedent. They also noted that Smith's decision presented itself as exemplary of our contemporary troubled times: they warned, in the words of Sopinka in *Rodriguez*, that the principles of fundamental justice "leave a great deal of scope for personal judgment:" the courts must be careful that fundamental justice is not interpreted as that which is "in the eye of the beholder *only*." The implication here was clear: Smith's judgment of Taylor's case was swayed with the subjectivism of the modern day "in the context of a society that demands and has enjoyed a greater degree of individual autonomy than ever before" (Paragraph 243). In response Newbury and Saunders claimed that despite this social shift:

> the societal consequences of permitting physician-assisted suicide in Canada—and indeed enshrining it as a constitutional right—are a matter of serious concern to many Canadians, and as is shown by the evidence reviewed by the trial judge in this case, no consensus on the subject is apparent, even among ethicists or medical practitioners.
>
> (Paragraph 243)

Newbury and Saunders' judgment brought the Taylor decision back into the folds of Sopinka's earlier claim that the protection of society's interests outweighed those of the individual.

Fundamental justice was, however, reconsidered in a later Supreme Court decision in *Carter v Canada* (Attorney General), 2015 SCC 5, [2015] 1 S.C.R. 331 in 2015. Despite Newbury and Saunders' efforts at overturning Smith, Chief Justice Beverley McLachlin—who we will remember had been a dissenting voice in Rodriguez's case and in favour of the right to die—stood by Smith's earlier claims and noted that:

> In order to demonstrate a violation of s.7, the claimants must first show that the law interferes with, or deprives them of, their life, liberty or security of the person. Once they have established that s.7 is engaged, they must then show that the deprivation in question is not in accordance with the principles of fundamental justice.
>
> (Paragraph 55)

This case concluded that:

> the prohibition on physician-assisted dying infringes upon the right to life, liberty and security of Ms. Taylor and of persons in her position, and that it does so in a manner that is overbroad and thus

> is not in accordance with the principles of fundamental justice. It therefore violates s.7.
>
> (Paragraph 56)

Thus, once again, fundamental justice was back to being considered "overbroad." To overcome the issue of societal interests, the case also noted that the claimant "should not be tasked with also showing that these principles are 'not overridden by a valid state or communal interest in these circumstances'" (Paragraph 80). Drawing from *R. v Swain* [1991] 1 S.C.R. 933, at page 977, the court noted that "It is not appropriate to thwart the exercise of the accused's right by attempting to bring societal interests into the principles of fundamental justice and to thereby limit the accused's s.7 rights. Societal interests are to be dealt with under s. 1 of the Charter" (Paragraph 80).

This here might be considered "affirmative:" by challenging the nature of the law being overbroad the case then noted that not every person appealing for the right to die must inevitably be deemed vulnerable. "There may be people with disabilities who have a considered, rational and persistent wish to end their own lives" (paragraph 86), it was noted and therefore "Canada argues that it is difficult to conclusively identify the 'vulnerable'" (Paragraph 87). Indeed, "Canada asserts that every person is potentially vulnerable from a legislative perspective" (Paragraph 87).

Despite the apparent headway made in Canadian law regarding the most recent case law challenge to the prospect that not all persons must be defined as vulnerable if they fall into particular categories of person—in the instance noted above, namely disabled—the law in England does not seem to follow suit.[2] Legal cases on assisted dying in England have also attended to the same point of tension between the state's interest in securing the wellbeing of society as a whole and the rights of the person to individual liberty but have come to a less "open" conclusion. Dianne Pretty's case, which was initially taken to the Director of Public Prosecutions in *R (Pretty) v Director of Public Prosecutions* [2001] UKHL 61, had sought to secure immunity for her husband such that he could help Pretty end her life without fear of being prosecuted. On denial of her case, Pretty took her appeal to the European Court of Human Rights in *Pretty v The United Kingdom* [2002] ECHR 427. Here the Court claimed that while it recognized and sympathized with Pretty—like Sopinka had done with regard to Rodriguez—the Court could not grant immunity to someone who would kill her because it was not considered compatible with the good of society: allowing assisted death did not comply with the laws that exist to preserve the "life and safety of others" (*Pretty v UK*, paragraph 74). The DPP argued that the right of the individual could be overruled when there arises a need to "balance" this right with "considerations of public health and safety against the countervailing principle of personal autonomy" (*Pretty v UK*, paragraph 74). The UK's 1961 Suicide Act Section 2 that prohibited assisted suicide was said to be grounded in this need to balance autonomy with the protection of the "weak and vulnerable and especially those who are not in a condition to take informed decisions against acts intended to end life or to assist in ending life." Likewise, as the House of Lords Select Committee noted in 1994, cited in *Pretty v UK*:

> Ultimately ... we do not believe that these arguments are sufficient reason to weaken society's prohibition of intentional killing. That prohibition is the cornerstone of law and of social relationships. It protects each one of us impartially, embodying the belief that all are equal. We do not wish that protection to be diminished and we therefore recommend that there should be no change in the law to permit euthanasia. We acknowledge that there are individual cases in which euthanasia may be seen by some to be appropriate. But individual cases cannot reasonably establish the foundation of a policy which would have such serious and widespread repercussions. Moreover, dying is not only a personal or individual affair. The death of a person affects the lives of others, often in ways and to an extent which cannot be foreseen. We believe that the issue of euthanasia is one in which the interest of the individual cannot be separated from the interest of society as a whole.
>
> (Paragraph 237)

From a similar vantage that Justice Lynn Smith had argued in the Taylor ruling, Pretty argued that this "balance" was entirely disproportionate (*Pretty v UK*, paragraph 45): Pretty's right was "an absolute one;" there could be no room for "balance." Societal interest could not outweigh her right given that this societal interest was only possible on the basis of a universal protection of individual rights.

Securing a Balance between the Interests of the Individual and Society

The chapter has thus far noted that legal cases on assisted dying invoke the concept of security in two ways: on the one hand the concept of security is invoked in the name of the person; on the other hand the concept of security is invoked in the name of society that protects the "whole" from the interests of the particular. In broad terms, legal discussions of assisted dying are framed as a "balance" of these interests. Scholars such as Pavlich (1996), Rose (1999), Donzelot and Gordon (2008) and Lemke (2011) have argued that the concept of security is frequently used, not only in discussions of assisted dying but also elsewhere, to enunciate a logic of governance that attempts to settle disputes between individuals as part of the collective body, or in this instance of legal cases on assisted dying between individuals and the idea of what constitutes the collective. Pavlich (2000) for instance notes the overlap here with what Foucault (2003) had called a "pastoral" model of governance. The pastoral model operates on the basis of the relationship between the one and the many, whereby it is vital for legal processes to reconcile the good of the individual with the good of the whole. Indeed this reconciliation between the one and the many has occupied a place in much of Foucault's later work on political rationalities of governance, particularly with regard to liberalism and neoliberalism, which share remnants of pastoral logics of power. As Foucault himself noted with reference to political liberalism and later neoliberalism, "I think the main characteristic of our political rationality is that this integration of the individuals in a community or in a totality results from a constant correlation between an increasing individualization and the reinforcement of this totality" (Foucault, 1988: 161–162).

As this book has already argued, following the insights of Foucault and Esposito, a pastoral logic of power in neoliberalism that endeavors to integrate the governance of the one and many has not dissipated but rather has intensified in the contemporary context. This intensification has been conceptualized via the legal fictions of the immune person and immune society, both of which aim to further dissociate subjects from one another to bring to fruition a neoliberal dream of a reciprocally dissociated society in which individuals share in common only their non-obligation and non-interference with one another. What comes to be regarded as a social good and what "secures" society in the current neoliberal era is that individuals operate as isolated subjects who are private, proper, persons and who do not interfere with other private, proper persons. As such, to secure the society one must also secure the subjects comprising this society: "Against the boundlessness of the community, which is *absoluta* and *exlege*, the individual and the state are born under the sign of separation and autonomy with regard to what is internal to their own proper borders," Esposito writes (2013:

128). Like the previous chapters noted of the way the law constructed concepts of enmity, vulnerability and inviolability to feed legal fictions of private, bordered persons, so too does the law use the concept of security to push us to withdraw, appropriate and remove us from what is common. "Only this division of what is common is able to give security to modern men and women," notes Esposito (2013: 128).[3]

In what follows I give two specific examples that emerge in assisted dying legal cases on how the concepts of security of persons and security of society appears to present a "balance of interests" while at the same time feeding, constructing and maintaining its two key legal fictions of the immune person and immune society, sometimes seen as being in contradiction with one another. The first example is the differentiation that law makes between positive and negative obligations, whereby it rationalizes the latter as that which feeds the fiction of the immune society. The second example is the differentiation the law makes between what it calls "security interests" and "liberty interests" of the person. The law calls on the concept of security to argue that only the former, security interests, is compatible with a neoliberal rationality of governance that requires that law feeds the fiction of the immune society which the latter, liberty interests, would otherwise threaten. Where liberty is seen to tip in favor of the individual at the expense of society, security is said to favor both.

Positive Obligations and Non-Interference

Within assisted dying legal cases, the concept of a "positive obligation" as opposed to a "negative obligation" was used to construct a legal fiction of the immune person who ought to be brought into the folds of the immune society. In much the same way that Chapter 3 noted that the law drew on a difference between positive acts and negative omissions (framed through non-interference), so too did the law make a similar distinction regarding a logic of non-interference in the case of these obligations. Specifically, when plaintiffs appealed to the legal concept of the "security of the person" in order to articulate their right to be assisted in death, the law denied these requests with reference to a difference between a positive obligation and a negative obligation. The law claimed that it did not owe a positive obligation to help persons die, but rather simply owed a negative obligation to ensure that persons were protected from one another. Much like inviolability feeding the fiction of the immune person who is protected from outside interference, the concept of security of persons was fashioned as a negative right that secured persons from outside interference but did not give such persons a right to demand anything further.

Consider the conditions outlined in *Pretty v DPP* [2001] by way of example. The judge, Lord Hope, drew on precedent set in *Rees v United Kingdom* [1986] 9 EHRR 56,[4] an earlier case that had dealt with the question as to whether a positive obligation existed for the state. *Rees* was a case of a female-to-male transsexual who after having undergone surgery and name change argued that the law was breaching his right to respect for private life and the right to marry. The case noted in its judgment that in order to determine:

> whether a negative or positive obligation exists, regard must be had to the fair balance that has to be struck between the general interest of the community and the interests of the individual, the search for which balance is inherent in the whole of the Convention.
>
> (Paragraph 37: 63–64)

The case then determined that the law owed no positive obligation to protect the private life of Rees; rather, the law simply had the negative obligation to protect Rees from outside interference: such protection did not mean that the state owed any intervention in terms of providing him provisions to marry.

Returning to *Pretty*, Lord Hope argued that the United Kingdom was not "under a positive obligation to ensure that a competent, terminally ill, person who wishes but is unable to take his or her own life should be entitled to seek the assistance of another without that other being exposed to the risk of prosecution" (Paragraph 15). Ultimately, Hope argued, following a precedent set in *Rees*, that a respect to a "private life" did not impose a positive obligation on the state to give the right to assisted suicide. *Pretty v UK* at paragraph 15 stated:

> Respect for a person's "private life", which is the only part of Article 8 which is in play here, relates to the way a person lives. The way she chooses to pass the closing moments of her life is part of the act of living, and she has a right to ask that this too must be respected. In that respect Mrs Pretty has the right of self-determination. In that sense, her private life is engaged even where in the face of terminal illness she seeks to choose death rather than life. But it is an entirely different thing to imply into these words a positive obligation to give effect to her wish to end her own life by means of an assisted

> suicide. I think that to do so would be to stretch the meaning of the words too far.

Not only did Justice Sopinka of *Rodriguez* make a similar differentiation between positive obligations and negative obligations but Sopinka also noted that a positive obligation that stipulated respect for an individual's security of person would conflict with the state's positive obligation to protect the life of all inviolable subjects under law. At paragraph 129 he stated "I find more merit in the argument that security of the person, by its nature, cannot encompass a right to take action that will end one's life as security of the person is intrinsically concerned with the well-being of the living person." This point was also made with regards to suicide: the judgment noted that while suicide was legalized in Canada in 1972 it was not actively encouraged; the state had no obligation to actively help subjects commit suicide. Suicide was a negative right to the non-interference from a paternal state, rather than a positive right conferred upon subjects. The state argued that it did not "advocate" suicide.

The concept of security is formed through this differentiation between positive and negative obligations; it feeds a legal fiction of an immune society that reflects a neoliberal political rationality grounded in a lack of obligations toward the other. Indeed, Hirschl (2000) notes that in a neoliberal era negative rights are far more likely to be guaranteed in law than positive obligations. This differentiation maps neatly onto the negative pole of what Esposito calls *immunitas* that refers only to the negative: "non-dominion, non-constriction, and non-community" (2011: 53). The legal judgments in the cases of *Pretty* and *Rodriguez* legitimate law's denial of assisted dying on the basis that the law has no need to *positively interfere* with subject's rights unless these rights are harming another subject under the law. Even though this protection from harm is articulated positively (i.e. the law articulates itself on the grounds of taking "active" steps to prevent harm to other persons), such protection from harm is articulated very much by way of a negative modality of immunization that operates on the basis of non-interference and the very protection of this non-interference. In short, law takes "positive" steps to secure freedom for persons *from* other persons: law takes positive steps to feed a legal fiction of a totality of immune persons—an immune society.

Put simply, the law articulates a positive obligation to protect persons from harm by articulating this positive obligation within the semantic framework of non-obligation: it does not aim to help people live in a state of solidarity, but rather it aims to help people live securely from the threat of other people. Therefore, the political rationality of governance that the concept of security reflects defines a double closure from communal obligations toward others. The concept of security does so first by appearing to provide a "positive obligation" to protect other lives of the whole community (the society) by securing this community via a "negative obligation" whereby the relations between subjects of the whole society are normalized according to a simultaneous non-interference with one another. Second, the concept of security closes off assisted dying appeals by way of denying the state's and law's positive obligation to actively bring about or help someone die by stating that there is no positive obligation to end life; there is only a positive obligation to protect it from outsiders. This legal decision therefore denies assisted dying appeals as it enunciates a neoliberal political rationality that is grounded in and reinforced through the non-interference of subjects. Via the concept of security operating in assisted dying cases the legal decision to deny assisted dying reflects a political rationality that ensures that subjects are divided from one another.

Here one can again draw a parallel between the differentiation between positive and negative obligations made through legal judgment with reference to security, and the differentiation between passive and active forms of killing formulated through the legal judgment explored in the previous Chapter 3 with reference to inviolability. Arguably both reveal how different concepts—inviolability and security—are used to feed legal fictions of bordered subjects that close persons off from the outside, highlighting law's lack of interference not as an infraction of justice or a thwarting of liberty but as its very protector (Nedelsky, 2012). In Chapter 3 this mechanism of drawing boundaries around individual subjects allowed law to personalize Bland and other subjects of law who remained under law's protection even though these subjects (and or those acting on their behalf) claimed such protection was also destructive. By invoking the concept of security as a freedom from others, or the right not to be interfered with (the appellant) and the right not to interfere (hence no positive obligation of the law), we see the reflections of a political rationality that seems to close off responsibility toward other subjects—both closing off the responsibility from the state toward appellants and also closing off the interference of the state in dictating the course of one's life from the vantage of the appellant.

Security Versus Liberty

The law also made another differentiation that helped feed the legal fictions of the immune society and immune person that together mirror a political rationality grounded in reciprocal non-interference. This second differentiation was between what the law called "security interests" versus "liberty interests." In *Rodriguez*, for instance, Sopinka used the concept of security to feed a legal fiction of the immune society as that which had at its core the best interests of all; in comparison, he used a parallel concept of liberty to feed a legal fiction of a non-immune person and a non-immune society whereby persons were free to pursue their own individual interests that would threaten the legal fiction of the immune society and would also in turn threaten the very possibility of the immune person: he said that Rodriguez's claim to be "free from governmental interference in making fundamental personal decisions concerning the terminal state of her life" was not considered a "security" interest but rather "only the liberty interest" (*Rodriguez*, paragraph 124).[5]

Arguably Sopinka made this distinction between security and liberty interests for the strict purpose of supporting his earlier denial of a positive obligation to protect the individual subject's interests in favor of simply protecting the subject from non-interference. Liberty was invoked as a concept that threatened to undo security. Liberty was attached to the depiction (or fiction) of a self-directing individual who would demand that the law provide him or her positive rights, which would mean the state and law would have to intervene with individuals to protect these rights. By linking liberty with positive rights in this way, the law then freed up security as simply a negative obligation. This allowed the law to deny the security of persons as a positive right and maintain security of persons as a negative right that could be folded within the security of society, as a negative obligation. The differentiation between negative and positive obligations allowed the law to separate liberty from security, framing the former as a positive obligation that would conflict with the greater good of society, and framing the latter as a negative obligation, allowing the security of persons to be folded within the security of society, upholding the legal fictions of the immune person and immune society. Were liberty, as it is articulated as a distinct concept in legal cases with reference to a positive obligation to protect individual rights, to be deemed an acceptable and necessary concept in law, it would feed a legal fiction not of an immune society but of a society that imposed positive obligations onto subjects. The concept of liberty would feed a fiction of a society of reciprocally bound individuals within a reciprocally bound society that aims to protect the liberties of each in positive obligatory ways. In Esposito's terms it might be more akin to an originary *munus*. This is contrasted to the negative concept of security that instead fixes law's goal as that which secures non-interference through negative obligations, and in turn feeds the legal fiction of the secure and immune society. Liberty is articulated as a dangerous concept in legal cases: it is a concept that is privative but not bordered; it is articulated as though it were in favor of the one, but not also of the totality.

Security, though articulated as a negative obligation, certainly imposes a positive obligation onto us as much as liberty and the protection of individual interest does. In alleging to govern less, a neoliberal rationality of governance does not refrain from interference (i.e. it does not stop taking positive steps to interfere); rather, it changes how it interferes by conducting conduct in different ways. In this regard, the concept of the security of society is drawn on and constructed in legal cases as the good society, and law is used as a discourse and technology of governance to bring this good society to realization (Barry *et al.*, 1996; Foucault, 1991a, 2003, 2009; Gordon, 1991; Rose, 1993, 1999, 2001). Indeed, as noted throughout this book, law became a technique of governance that also operated more and more as a norm and as a conduit of the political rationality of governance. Expanding on François Ewald's (1986, 1990) thesis on the social function of law one might note that the law operated through reference to the social custom as a "norm." The very goal of social law is to make each individual feel "secure" (Zamboni, 2008). Cases on assisted dying construct concepts of security of society in opposition to concepts of personal securities (that are not liberties) in order to present an alleged seamless balance between the individual and the collective good. On the basis of this we can posit as Ewald did that "Judging in terms of balance means judging the value of an action or a practice in terms of its relationship to social normality, in terms of those customs or habits which at a certain moment are those of a given group" (Ewald, 1986: 68). In this event, judging in terms of balance means finding a way to ensure that legal judgments on assisted dying bring into effect the legal fiction of the secure society that can outweigh by folding within itself the legal fiction of the secure person, the latter of which is not an individual who is "alone" and self interested merely by way of his or her liberty but instead is only self interested by virtue of his or her larger connection to the secure society: one cannot be an immune person without also being a member of the immune society. Returning to Rodriguez's case, Sopinka made this clear. He referred to the concept of security as that which encompassed both the security of persons and the security of society, while he referred to the concept of liberty (that which cannot be entertained in law) as that which only encompassed an individualized element, and that which would threaten the prospect of a unified whole.

This neoliberal governance corresponds with what Esposito (2012c) terms both the "defensive" and "offensive" barriers of immunity. We might think of these as parallel to the negative and positive liberties that neoliberalism invokes, such that the former, negative liberty, is a defensive barrier drawn between the self and other that asserts an imperative for non-interference, and the latter, positive liberty, is an offensive strategy employing law and rights, framed through the concept of self-mastery. These, as Esposito posits, are two sides of the same immunized mechanism of defense and protection whereby "both emerge within a negative horizon of meaning" (2008: 70–71). Here Esposito means that both negative and positive liberties are ways of withdrawing from the affirmative obligation of the community. Both "types" of liberty—positive and negative—expressly have the same function, which is to close off the parameters around the self through security and privatization. The neoliberal immune community simply articulates itself as one that is comprised of negative rights, obligations and omissions to create a fiction of an immune society, despite it also shaping this society positively in the way it sees fit according to its own set of norms. In constituting liberty as a contradiction of the good immune society, the prospect of assisted dying remains framed within a political rationality of governance that does the work of shoring up the limits of human relationships: law frames assisted dying as a positive act of killing, much like the previous chapter noted. To assist with someone's death is to take positive steps of intervention that would burden and threaten the security of other persons who exist outside one's self. The legal decision to deny assisted dying through the generation of the concept of security of society feeds the legal fiction of the neoliberal immune society; our relations to one another are continually bound to a condition of reciprocal independence in which we owe no positive obligation toward one another but rather owe a negative obligation: we must not interfere.

Our modern horizon of freedom (i.e., what we can do and how we can live) is "immunized" through the concept of security.[6] As such, the legal fiction of the immune person inscribed within the immune society privatizes us in two ways: "It is privatized *and* deprives us of that relation which exposes it to its communal mark" (Esposito 2008: 61, emphasis added). For Esposito, this means "the individual appears protected from the negative border that makes him himself and not the other" (2008: 61). As with the previous two chapters, the concept of security highlights how the law divides individuals from one another through concepts that establish fictional limits between subjects. We can see a conceptual analogy to Esposito's philosophical notion of immunity and community: where freedom in *communitas* was a reciprocal freedom through a common debt, freedom in *immunitas* remains reciprocal through the non-obligation or dispensation from this debt. While the dispensation from the *munus* is typically granted on the basis of privilege, the liberal—and increasingly neoliberal—operation of freedom demands that this freedom be considered universal, such that *all* members of the community—now properly defined—receive a dispensation, and are no longer obligated to one another. Everyone, no matter whether privileged or not, is alleged to be "free," or have the capacity to be so, on the basis of this universal immunity that (neo)liberal democracy proclaims to grant. Esposito writes:

> When, beginning with Hobbes as the model of natural law, modern political philosophy attempts to restore universality to the concept of freedom, it can only do so within an individualistic framework that has now been extended and multiplied by the number of individuals who are made equal by their reciprocal separation. Freedom is what separates the self from the other by restoring it to the self; it's what heals and rescues the self from every common alteration.
>
> (Esposito, 2012c: 53–54)

This is precisely the aporia revealed in legal appeals to assisted death: cases of Rodriguez, Taylor, Pretty and others point to an immunitary mechanism whereby their liberty, framed as a necessary privatization and preservation of the individual subject is seen to contradict the preservation of the whole of which this subject is said to be a part. Liberty does not feed a fiction of an immune person within an immune society: it feeds a fiction of an immune subject that must be deconstructed in law because its immunity would threaten the tenets of the immune society.

Dangers of an Immune Society

Two problems are revealed through the legal fiction of the immune society that folds within itself the immune person as a necessary and conforming part of this whole. First, it legitimates closures around subjects such that secure individual subjects are no longer obligated toward one another but rather have become increasingly secure from one another and more and more dissociated. This is consistent with Esposito's thesis that immunity mechanisms have a "continual recourse to create ever more extensive and intensive security-producing dispositifs" (Esposito and Paparcoe, 2006: 55). Second, it legitimates the immunization of each and all such that the immunization of each often resultantly occurs as part of a governmental immunization of all. The individual comes to desire a closing off of their own self that operates in potentially destructive ways for the good of this whole such that mechanisms of protection often end up causing the individual to sacrifice themselves, rationalizing and legitimating a kind of violence.

In an excellent genealogy and philology of "security" John Hamilton (2013: 81) notes this very problem: "Security grants identity but seals this achievement with a gravestone. Proponents of a human care that does not seek resolution in care's removal recognise that the subject is sacrificed to the very institutions that make the subject a subject." Ultimately Hamilton touches upon an aporia of security. He notes that the problem with the appeal to the security of the individual (as *singulatum*) that is part of a governance agenda that aims to also secure the whole (*omnes*) is that the self will always necessarily sacrifice itself to this greater whole. One cannot be a "self" without this whole (Esposito, 2010; Lopez, 2013). Esposito notes for example that individuals are "paradoxically sacrificed to their own survival" (2010: 14). Likewise Lopez adds: "Extirpating every living bond, every trace of a shared and henceforth exposed existence, Law demands the sacrifice of life itself in exchange for its protection" (2013: 21). While neoliberal political rationalities might operate discursively through conduits such as law to bring into being legal fictions that operate as security mechanisms, and these might provide us with the prospect of a subjective identity (the fiction of the immune person who is self-directing, bordered and absolutely sovereign), in their very process of conferring upon us this security or immunity, that is in removing us from what Hamilton calls a reciprocal "care" or what Esposito calls "*munus*," or what one might simply call an openness and exposure to otherness—in removing us from the positive obligation to others or what necessarily takes us outside of ourselves precluding the possibility of self in *communitas*—the very *possibility* of the individual that is granted necessarily in establishing it *qua* individual becomes sacrificed to the law that secures immunity, the new "immune community"—the *omnes,* the "whole."

A lesson from this is as follows: we ought to be cautious of how an appellant seeking assisted death frames his or her appeal through a desire for personal security that is consistent with the logic of the security of the state. Even when the law claims that these two things are contradictory, what we see emerge is an individual who seeks to secure him or herself not simply *from* the larger community but *for the sake of* this community; not in the name of a reciprocal obligation to the other but in the name of a reciprocal independence from these others. We must therefore be cautious when the right to die appeal is symptomatic of a desire to secure oneself from the kind of dependent relations found in a community of reciprocal obligations that simply reifies the larger neoliberal political rationality grounded in divisions between subjects. A deconstruction of the legal fictions that feed off of these concepts of security allows us to rethink assisted dying away from security and immunization toward a different prospect of community.

Conclusion

This chapter has examined the concept of security as it emerged in right to die cases in two ways: first with reference to the security of society, and second with reference to the security of the person. The chapter suggested that the concept of security is articulated in legal judgments in such a way as to fix two objects of law that are both legal fictions. The first object of law is that of "society" itself or the very possibility that one can imagine society to share in common the goal of its own security on the basis of security as a social good: the fiction of the "immune society." The second object of law is that of the "secure person." By differentiating between positive and negative obligations, as well as security versus liberty interests, the law fixes the secure person as a part of the immune society: the fiction of the immune person who is folded within the immune society is maintained via the assertion that these two fictions are inseparable. Security of persons is folded within the security of society through a legal fiction of an immune society comprised of absolutely immune persons, which presents these two concepts of security as necessarily inscribed within one another; to further support this fiction, the law also draws on other concepts such as liberty and positive obligations that it articulates as dangerous to the legal fictions given that these concepts would undo the fictive relation between the one and the whole. The chapter argued that the fiction of their simultaneous operation allows the governmental rationality to bring the individual within the logic of the larger whole while presenting the legal decision as a balancing act that aims to secure the rights and freedoms of individuals only if they conform to the rights and freedoms of the good society.

In theorizing this balancing act of security the chapter drew more fully on Foucault's account of governmentality in conversation with Esposito's account of immunization, or what Oliva (2006) called the "immune community." In drawing these ideas together the chapter argued that we can read the current paradox of security in right to die appeals as symptomatic of—and enunciating of—the neoliberal political rationality that simultaneously brings us together and divides us, to the extent that what we hold "in common" is our freedom and security from one another: a common immunization. In view of this the chapter argued that the concept of security articulated in legal decisions on assisted dying and in legal appeals to assisted dying is highly problematic. The problem of liberalism, which is an increasing problem of neoliberalism (Campbell, 2011), is that:

> To the degree that it isn't limited to the simple enunciation of imperative of liberty but implicates the organization of conditions that make this effectively possible, liberalism contradicts its own premises. Needing to construct and channel liberty in a nondestructive direction for all of society, liberalism continually risks destroying what is wants to create.
>
> (Esposito, 2008: 74)

Law as a discourse and technology of governance that uses concepts of security to feed a legal fiction that serves to divide us from what is common comes at a price. It comes at the expense of always sacrificing the individual to the whole: the promise of an absolutely immune society of reciprocal independence will always find ways to rationalize the death or denial of rights to subjects who threaten the whole. In the previous chapter this was made possible by depersonalizing and allowing the law to operate as a norm through fictions that generated distinctions between acts and omissions; in this chapter this was apparent through differentiations between positive and negative obligations: both are fictive, and both attempt to divide us from obligations toward one another, rationalizing the possibility to ignore requests to die, or allowing some deaths on the basis of necessary fictions of division.

The next chapter turns to the concept of "dependency" which is bound within this same problematic of an individualizing, immunizing society that has shifted away from ideals of community expressed as an opening up of the borders of the self. It considers how the concept of dependency becomes attached to degeneracy and an abject social status. A key argument here is that the law does not challenge the association between dependency and degeneracy; instead it fixes the correlation through a concept of degeneracy that forms part of a legal fiction through which assisted death is denied. The chapter additionally considers how the assisted dying appellant appears to emerge as he or she who increasingly desires a freedom from dependent relations in ways that feed the same legal fictions and also fulfills the promise of a neoliberal immune community.

Notes

1 As Denike (2000: 153) writes, typically the principles of fundamental justice are enacted in line with the social norms that favor the "masculine," "liberal, abstract, universalist rule."

2 One might hesitate to make a more conclusive statement here given that the Canadian Supreme Court only very recently (2015) passed this judgment and Parliament has yet to formally respond to the decision.

3 According to Esposito (2008), one can consider the concept of liberty in its originary etymological meaning in association with the concept of the *munus*. From Esposito's etymological vantage, he noted that the concept of liberty (*libertates*) that we find in the *munus* or the space of reciprocal obligation referred to an "increase, a non-closing" (2008: 70). Its "original affirmative connotation" was thus one that could be articulated as being expansive; liberty united members of community in a sharedness of being (2008: 70).

4 *Rees v United Kingdom* [1986] 9 EHRR 56, paragraph 37 of its judgment at pages 63–64 stated the following:

> In determining whether or not a positive obligation exists, regard must be had to the fair balance that has to be struck between the general interest of the community and the interests of the individual, the search for which balance is inherent in the whole of the Convention. In striking this balance the aims mentioned in the second paragraph of Article 8 may be of a certain relevance, although this provision refers in terms only to "interferences" with the right protected by the first paragraph - in other words is concerned with the negative obligations flowing therefrom.

5 The full quote is here:

> The appellant argues that, by prohibiting anyone from assisting her to end her life when her illness has rendered her incapable of terminating her life without such assistance, by threat of criminal sanction, s. 241(b) deprives her of both her liberty and her security of the person. The appellant asserts that her application is based upon (a) the right to live her remaining life

> with the inherent dignity of a human person, (b) the right to control what happens to her body while she is living, and (c) the right to be free from governmental interference in making fundamental personal decisions concerning the terminal stages of her life. The first two of these asserted rights can be seen to invoke both liberty and security of the person; the latter is more closely associated with only the liberty interest.
>
> (Paragraph 124)

6 While we do see that communities of care are often forged despite this imperative not to interfere with the other, these care communities tend to replicate an instance of a "proper community" in that they allow us to determine who to respond to, rather than being reciprocally bound to respond to all others. One might consider here Derrida's (1995) caution whereby when one chooses to respond to an ethical demand there are a number of others one is equally *not* responding to. Thus, the ethical demand is immunized such that it forms the self *and* other through immunity (or sets up the host/hostis relation) (Derrida, 2000). In this sense, immunization makes it possible to justify attempts to care for family (should we choose to do so), or forge social care communities, which are also oftentimes exclusionary. We might open this discussion up further to consider who receives care, for instance.

Chapter 5

Freedom from Dependent Relations

Like the previous chapter that examined how subjects appealing for assisted dying and the law that denied these appeals both articulated a concept of security, this chapter considers both appellants' and the law's use of another concept, namely dependency. With reference to the former, the chapter focuses on how appeals to a "death with dignity," one of the most common phrases used by plaintiffs in assisted dying appeals, is best interpreted as a desire to be free from dependent relations with others. On this point, the chapter addresses the relation between indignity and dependency: the appellant's subjectivity is shaped through the neoliberal political rationality where the latter emphasizes that to be dignified is to be an independent subject who does not interfere with the independence of other subjects. In short, the appellant's articulation of the concept of dependency feeds the two legal fictions noted throughout of the bounded subject divorced from reciprocal relations of dependency within a larger immune society of independent persons.

Where subjects appeal to assisted death as a "right to die" based on a desire to be free from dependent relations, the law claims to protect subjects from the internalization of neoliberal norms, stating that appellants might feel a "duty to die." While the law appears benevolent when it denies assisted dying based on a concern that subjects have internalized a problematic ethos of being "dependents," the chapter argues the law does not try to remedy this internalization of an abject subject status so much as confirm and fix it by noting that appellants of assisted dying are particular kinds of subjects. Hence, the law does not undo the problematic relation between indignity and dependency that fixes particular subjects as the proper kind of appellant for death; rather, law continues to fix the appellants as particular kinds of people (elderly, disabled or terminally ill) who are all classified as dependents and are thereby undignified (i.e. persons who burden or obligate others). This means to suggest that the law does not challenge the social norms, such as the "fact" that certain kinds of people are legitimate in their appeals to death, which is shaped by the larger negative connotation of being a dependent in a society defined by an independent ethos; instead, the law simply, at present, shows a concern regarding the act of killing itself (i.e. how one "gets rid" of these dependents). It is this latter aspect of assisted dying appeals that do not comport with the overall legal fictions of the immune person and immune society and would thereby contradict the neoliberal ethos. In short, the law's denial of assisted dying appears to be paradoxical because it would seem that to let abject subjects be killed would be beneficial to the neoliberal immune community; however, when one looks beyond the *ratio decidendi* and examines law as a discourse enunciative of broader rationalities of governance one can note an underpinning immunizing logic whereby the law simply has not yet found a way to rationalize some kinds of assisted death within this immunizing logic. In turn, the chapter argues that if assisted death were to be rationalized, we ought to be concerned with precisely how this rationalization would occur, particularly if it were in accordance with the reciprocally divisive ethos of neoliberalism (as Chapter 3 for instance, highlighted with reference to the legitimation of Bland's death).

Death with Dignity: Freedom from Dependency

> She will be totally dependent upon machines to perform her bodily functions and completely dependent upon others. Throughout this time, she will remain mentally competent and able to appreciate all that is happening to her. Although palliative care may be available to ease the pain and other physical discomfort which she will experience, the appellant fears the sedating effects of such drugs and argues, in any event, that they will not prevent the psychological and emotional distress which will result from being in a situation of utter dependence and loss of dignity.

This above excerpt is taken from *Rodriguez* at paragraph 137, explaining her plight. Indeed, each of the assisted dying cases analyzed revealed similar assertions: most appellants, like Rodriguez, framed their appeals to assisted death based on the perceived failure and degeneracy of their body and how this failure would leave them in a state in which they were absolutely dependent on other persons. Appellants tended to argue that they wanted an assisted death for two, somewhat overlapping, reasons on the basis of this degeneracy. The first reason was that subjects did not want their person intruded upon such that they would be subject to outside interference—that is, they did not want to be dependent on others because this would impose on their own freedom as an individual. The second reason was that subjects did not want to burden their loved ones. While most appellants recognize their loved ones would be happy to look after and care for them, the appellants typically felt that this would impose too great an obligation onto them. In both of these instances, appellants sought what they called a "death with dignity."

While scholars have discussed the various meanings of dignity in death and have debated the ethics of dignity as a concept (e.g., Dworkin *et al.*, 1997; Waldron, 2009),[1] when one examines the wording of cases one notes that dignity is used in a very specific way:[2] in legal cases on assisted dying a death with dignity is best described as life that is freed from dependent relations through death. This uptake of the term "death with dignity" in legal appeals creates a clear link between an undignified life and a dependent life, and thereby a dignified death and an independent death: one is not dignified in either life or death if one is dependent on others. This is entirely consistent with critical disability theorist, Susan Behuniak's, commentary. She claims that while the concept of dignity is polyvalent, it appears most readily in assisted dying legal appeals as a way to legitimate a "liberation from indignity" (2011: 18). In assisted dying appeals, this appeal to a death with dignity conceptualizes death as a liberation from the indignities of illness, and/or disability (where often disability is considered synonymous with illness) (Oliver, 1990). While appellants used the concept of dignity to express their desire to die, within the legal cases this concept of dignity referred most specifically to a desire not to be dependent. The prospect of liberation from indignities that Behuniak noted is more precisely articulated in assisted dying cases as a liberation from dependent relations.

Problematic dependent relations were articulated in two further ways in the assisted dying cases examined: the first was with reference to the failing body that could no longer do the things it used to do; the second was with reference to the way this failing body relied on technology and other forms of care from others that would intervene with the body and that would intervene with the freedom of others who would be burdened by this care. As noted in the excerpt from Rodriguez's case, she had feared that her body would be reliant on machines and on others who would care for her: she would be absolutely dependent.

Nicklinson's case expressed a similar fear. Recalling his plea noted earlier in Chapter 2, he claimed emphatically:

> My life can be summed up as dull, miserable, demeaning, undignified and intolerable ... it is misery created by the accumulation of lots of things which are minor in themselves but, taken together, ruin what's left of my life. Things like ... constant dribbling; having to be hoisted everywhere; loss of independence, ... particularly toileting and washing, in fact all bodily functions (by far the hardest thing to get used to); having to forgo favourite foods; ... having to wait until 10:30 to go to the toilet ... in extreme circumstances I have gone in the chair, and have sat there until the carers arrived at the normal time.
>
> (*Nicklinson v MOJ*, 2012, paragraph 13)

In his mind, what Nicklinson described was an unbearable existence and one that he would rather not live through. Life was considered undignified on the basis of what he perceived to be an absolute relation of dependency to his physical existence and to others that he was confined to: dependent relations infantilized and dehumanized him; these relations constrained him to a body that he could not care for or control himself, whereby he would dribble or defecate in his chair; he was subjected to the necessary care (and interference) of others, being absolutely reliant on others for "private" tasks such as toileting. From Nicklinson's vantage the law's refusal to allow him to die confined him to a life of dependency and indignity. Nicklinson sought a freedom from a corporeality that he conceived as exposing of his self to outsiders and dependent relations (e.g., Fennell, 2004; Hepworth, 1996).

Norms and Dependency

Appeals to assisted death are shaped by social norms (Mihic, 2008; Tierney, 2006). Social norms tell us that to be dependent on others is undesirable (Amundson and Taira, 2005). In a neoliberal context this is especially so as indicated by a considerable rise in appeals to assisted death since the 1970s (Lavi, 2008). What and who is said to constitute a dependent subject is socially constructed and is shaping of and shaped by the political rationality of the time (Biggs and Powell, 2001). For instance, the welfare state is more likely to accept ageing dependents (e.g., Townsend, 1981; Walker, 1982) whereas a neoliberal entrepreneurial state is more likely to consider such persons' worth (as a discursively constituted category of "elderly") on the basis of a perceived lack of human capital (Powell, 2001). This is particularly the case as the neoliberal capitalist state has conferred more responsibility onto families and individuals themselves for dealing with the processes of ageing (Powell, 2001; Powell and Biggs, 2003).

Here we can also draw a link to points raised throughout to suggest that political rationalities of governance play a large role in shaping perceptions of what constitutes a "dependent" person—that is, who is said to be a dependent subject. Ageing has come to be viewed and assessed within a bio-medical model that gets attached to decline, degeneracy, abnormality and dependency and is therefore regarded as a "problem" (Biggs and Powell, 2001; Phillipson, 1998). The same can be said for disability whereby the use of the concept of dependency linked to degeneration details a truth about living with a disability.

Scholars like Shelly Tremain (2005) have argued that abelist discourses in society contribute to a normalization of the body such that disability is "medicalized" and considered an "illness" of individuals. In an era where one's worth is measured by one's productive output, the association between disability, degeneracy and dependency in the same way as ageing also serves to contribute to the narrative of disability as an individual problem that affects the larger social fabric (Saltes, 2013). We see here that the individualized "problem" of disability where it is deemed undesirable to live with a disability or an illness or aging issues is also intimately associated with social values of disability. That is, disability is not only an individual problem whereby subjects ought to desire to become normal on the basis of ablest norms (McRuer, 2006; Tremain, 2005) that allow said subjects to live more independently as divided and immunized selves, but also that subjects with disabilities are articulated as dependent, and therefore a burden, on society (McWhorter, 2005; Tremain, 2005). Disabled persons are seen to interfere with other subject's personal rights and immunity because their disability causes them to "take" from the liberal state (Lero *et al.*, 2012; Pothier and Devlin, 2006; Saltes, 2013; Taylor, 2011; Waldschmidt, 2006).

Immune Persons

One might argue that appeals to death with dignity invoked on the grounds of a desire to be free from dependent relations simply feed the same legal fiction of the immune person that appellants claim to want protection from. Appellants reify the existing neoliberal political rationality that constructs them as particular kinds of subjects (degenerates). Rodriguez and Nicklinson's appeals to assisted death used the concept of dependency to feed a legal fiction of the immune person as he or she who ought to be protected from these dependent relations that were articulated as relations that consisted of too much outside interference. Nicklinson, for instance, had appealed to a personal immunity from outside intrusion that he regarded as infantilizing, dehumanizing and paternalistic because it forced him to remain in an absolutely dependent relationship with others (i.e. caregivers).

Such an express desire to be free from dependent relations is arguably complicit with the neoliberal political ethos of "reciprocal independence" discussed throughout this book. The desire to free oneself from dependent relations reinforces the legal fictions of immune persons and an immune society that reflect a neoliberal rationality that demands increasing independence of subjects from one another. A death with dignity, which at once constitutes one as a proper subject (self directing), and also releases one as a proper subject from a relation of dependence with others, is not possible without the legal fiction of an immune person who is sovereign over him or herself, free from relations with and to others. One might say, as Feinberg (1986: 354) does, that a death with dignity is "not possible without the acknowledgement of personal sovereignty." Sovereignty in this sense is the articulation of a type of personalization; it is the constitution of the proper person as a subject of law who can appeal to the right to a "proper" death, which is dignified because it treats the subject as a proper person who is not interfered with by others. It also does not treat the subject simply as a "thing" that can be controlled by others; one is a thing not a person if one is dependent on others. To be a person is to dictate one's will; to be a thing is to have no will but rather be subject to the will of others. Assisted dying appeals are attempts to turn the self from a thing that cannot be mastered efficiently through bodily processes and that is subsequently dependent on relations with others to sustain one's self, into a "person" who can be mastered rationally through the exercise of free will: subjects appeal to their own sovereignty and personalization in order to refute their alleged corporeal degeneracy; in doing so they claim to assert sovereign control over their body and an independence from the paternalistic decisions of others. A dignified, proper death is not dehumanizing and infantilizing as Nicklinson's case had earlier depicted; rather, it is a death that is free from dependent relations. An assisted death that would allow someone to help Nicklinson die in a way that would free him from relations of dependency would be a good death.

The notion of a proper death or a "good death" being one in which the subject retains his or her proper status through personalization—hence, one in which the subject maintains a personal sovereignty or control over his or her body and actions—arguably mimics the desire for sovereignty as a "whole" and independent being. Nicklinson's case articulated depersonalization as that which is associated with dependency, calling it infantilizing and animalizing. His case reinforced that the good death had to conform to social norms of personhood that also required independence: to die well is to die as an independent person. Here one can draw a parallel to the concept of inviolability of persons discussed in Chapter 3 of this book: a dignified death is a death that seeks to shore up and feed a legal fiction of an immune person who is a proper person such that his or her body cannot be interfered with by outsiders. The appellant, through his or her appeal to a freedom from dependent relations with others via assisted death, produces himself or herself as a bounded subject (Nedelsky, 1990), feeding the legal fiction of the immune person.

Where appellants have endeavored to become a person through law and have fed a legal fiction of an immune person who is protected from outsiders by claiming their right to die with dignity as a rational, adult, sovereign human rather than as a subject who is dehumanized and infantilized through dependent relations, two key problems emerge. The first problem emerges when one equates dependency with indignity. As noted previously, this has the effect of relating particular subject positions that are deemed to be dependent with an undignified life (Oliver, 1996). This also has the effect of fixing "who" can appeal to assisted death: only those who are sufficiently degenerate (understood as those who are absolutely dependent on others and perceived as undignified) can be the proper subjects of assisted death. When one fixes the subjectivity for assisted death this also means that subjects who want to appeal to death have to sufficiently fulfill this subject position; it means that Nicklinson, for instance, cannot simply claim that he wants someone to help him die, but also that he must declare absolutely his dependent status in order to be considered the correct type of person for assisted death. To appeal for assisted death requires in the first instance a depersonalization before a subject can then claim a personalization via an appeal to self-direction and a freedom from this dependent status. Only by effectively fixing one's corporeality can a subject then distance him or herself from this corporeality through acts of personalization by creating legal fictions of an immune person who is independent, sovereign and able to exercise the self as free from dependent relations when making this decision. However, through this personalization, the subject also fixes his or her corporeality as a sovereign individual: in doing so the subject becomes "inviolable" and therefore an immune person who cannot receive the assistance in death that is sought. It seems somewhat of a paradox: at once a personalization is sought in order to become sovereign and independent; yet in doing so the subject then requires a dependent death via assistance from another which is subsequently denied to immune persons.

This fixing of subject positions is a key part of the problem with assisted dying appeals. It is only on the basis that the appellant for assisted dying disqualifies his or her life in accordance with social norms (i.e. that one accepts that one is not normal and that one's life is not worth living because it is dependent, which goes against the norm) that one can legitimately appeal for assisted death. Appealing to die with dignity uses the indignity of dependent relations to try to erase the trace of this indignity through a personalized, independent death. In doing so, one's "dignified death" arguably does not sever the more apparent link that binds degeneracy to dependency and thus to indignity in the first instance. An appeal to a dignified death as a sovereign, independent death also places the appellant in a bind whereby their personalization feeds the fiction of the immune person thus precluding the very possibility of the assisted death that they seek. I will return to this point later with more specific reference to the operation of law and will explain how the law appears to act benevolently in protecting subjects yet does not challenge and deconstruct the social norms that link degeneracy to dependency as much as it reinforces these norms. For now I will continue to focus on the appellants and their requests for assisted death that invoke the concept of dependency which feeds a legal fiction of an immune society.

Immune Society

Thus far the chapter has argued that the appeal to a death with dignity as that death which is free from dependent relations feeds a legal fiction of an immune person. It has been argued that this is consistent with other chapters in the book where concepts have emerged in legal cases on assisted dying to feed the legal fiction of the immune person as the bordered sovereign independent subject; this in turn precludes the prospect of assisted death that is said to otherwise contradict this fiction. The beginning of this section also noted another way that appellants also invoked the concept of dependency, this time with more specific reference to the impact one's dependent self would have on others who would be burdened by one's care. Here one can take Gloria Taylor's case as an example.

In 2012, Gloria Taylor's plea for the right to die was met with what many pro-right to die activists would regard as a "success:" she was granted a constitutional exemption from Canadian law and was allowed the right to have a physician assist with her death should she indicate a point in time in which her life was beyond tolerable. The judge, Justice Lynn Smith, framed Taylor's appeal in the following way:

> Ms. Taylor's illness is steadily impacting her ability to do … things. She is fearful about the progression of her disease and about which of her body's functions will be affected next. She says that one of her greatest fears is to be reduced to a condition where she must rely on others for all of her needs. She does not wish "to live in bedridden state, stripped of dignity and independence."
>
> (*Carter v Canada*, 2012, paragraph 52)

As Taylor stated in her own words:

> I want to be very clear: I do not believe that my family considers me a burden. Nor am I concerned that as I get more and more ill they will begin to do so. When I told my family and friends that I wanted a physician-assisted death, my concern was that they might be disappointed in me for not trying to hold on and stay with them until the last possible moment. But I do want to express the fact that I, myself, will be greatly distressed by living in a state where I have no function or functionality that requires others to attend to all of my needs and thereby effectively oblige my family to bear witness to the final steps of the process of my dying with the indignity a slow death from ALS will entail. I do not, in particular, want to be the cause of my 11 year old granddaughter's sitting vigil as I die an ugly death, and I believe that is what she will do, because she loves me. I do not want to be a burden, not because I fear my family does or would resent me—I do not think that—rather, I do not want to be a burden because I know they love me.
>
> (*Carter v Canada*, 2012, paragraph 52)

Justice Smith drew on a plethora of ethical, legal, medical and psychological expertise to present the case set forth. One particular source was Ganzini *et al.*'s (2008) research on depression and assisted suicide, which supported the quote from Taylor. Following interviews with over 50 patients, Ganzini *et al.* noted: "Although many worry about being a burden, in fact, their families would appreciate the opportunity to give greater care. These are very independent people who do not want more care" (Cited in *Carter v Canada,* 2012, paragraph 438). Given Taylor's assertions, and those put forth by Ganzini *et al.*, the principal issue at stake in Taylor's appeal to the right to die did not seem to be whether she would be conceived as a dependent and therefore a burden. Rather, what seemed to be more centrally at stake was the notion that Taylor, herself, refused a position of becoming a dependent: she did not want to become dependent on her family who she noted would have happily cared for her but who would have inevitably been burdened by this care.

In Taylor's case she articulated her appeal to die not only on the grounds that she desired a freedom for the right to her own self-direction or positive freedom as an individual, but also because she was heavily aware of not implicating her loved ones. She denied being fearful that another person would take her life (or so she said); she also denied being fearful that her family members would resent her or see her as an obligation. She was not, at least outwardly, concerned with a reduction of herself to the status of a thing, or an abject other as Esposito and others like Mihic (2008) and Tierney (2006) have suggested as a possibility. Ganzini *et al.*'s remarks also seemed to support this rationale. However, Taylor still refused to obligate her family, framing her desire for an assisted death as a release of her loved one's from this obligation. In this sense one can see a more overt fiction of the immune society being fed via an appeal to die for the sake of preserving (indeed immunizing) the other's freedom from dependent relations toward oneself. In short, it is not simply that the legal appeals to a death that is free from dependency feed a legal fiction of an immune person who is free from interference from others, but also that appeals to death attempt to help secure the freedom of others from whom one endeavors to be free. It thus brings to bear how the two legal fictions overlap with the individualizing and totalizing poles of pastoral power in neoliberal rationalities of governance, discussed most extensively in Chapter 4: appellants want to free themselves from dependent relations, but they also want to free the other from these relations to which they would obligate them. Through an immunizing logic of closure the individual invariably sacrifices himself or herself to the whole.

Law's Denial of Appeals to Freedom from Dependent Relations

I have argued that the law continues to deny assisted dying, despite appeals to the right to die as a "freedom from dependency" appearing to feed the same legal fictions that the law purports. If the appeals are complicit with the legal fictions, why does the law refuse them? This section of the chapter focuses on two things. First, it notes how the law appears to act benevolently based on a concern that subjects have internalized a problematic ethos of dependency. That is, the chapter focuses on the law's construction of the subjects of assisted death as dependent subjects who would necessarily feel compelled to die. Second, it focuses on the problem of law's benevolence: it argues that its claim to benevolence via a paternalism is problematic because the law presents itself as a mechanism of protection that does not try to remedy this internalization of an abject status so much as confirm and fix it by noting that appellants of assisted dying are particular kinds of subjects.

Law's Benevolence

The law presents itself in assisted dying cases as a benevolent and paternal force; it claims to protect subjects from the internalization of social norms that frame subjects who are dependent on others as abject and vulnerable. Because of this dependent status, as Chapter 2 on enmity and vulnerability noted, the law claims it must protect subjects from other persons who would likely kill the abject subjects because the latter would interfere with the freedom of the former. Likewise, the law presents the vision that appellants, being particular kinds of persons, would inevitably (indeed universally so) feel pressured to seek out actively or succumb to the social pressure to die in a way that the society sees fit. In paragraph 89 of *Rodriguez*, this was the point communicated by Lamer (dissenting):

> Sadly, increasingly less value appears to be placed in our society on the lives of those who, for reason of illness, age or disability, can no longer control the use of their bodies. Such sentiments are often, unfortunately, shared by persons with physical disabilities themselves, who often feel they are merely a burden and expense to their families or on society as a whole.

Indeed, in the current neoliberal era whereby privacy has extended beyond the family unit to the individual self, being dependent on one's family and friends is considered increasingly burdensome (Biggs and Powell, 2000). Biggs and Powell (2000) for instance point to the rise of "elder abuse" in the contemporary society to argue that we are increasingly finding ourselves desiring freedom from dependent relations that obligate us to others, including from relations that obligate us to our own families. Others also point to the decline in social responsibility toward elderly persons within western societies, romanticizing eastern cultures for their respect for elders, and criticizing individualizing western cultures for their treatment and disregard of elders whose value have come to be associated with a mere drain on public and private resources (Kenner, 2008; Pfaff *et al.*, 2010).

Mihic (2008) for instance notes that in the era of neoliberalism persons might be coerced toward choosing death rather than burdening their families given the prospect of exponential medical bills. The neoliberal subject is never free or autonomous but is moulded and shaped "to fit the socio-economic order in the form of human capital" (Mihic, 2008: 167). Mihic continues: "advocates of physician assisted suicide conceive of the self as human capital" (2008: 170). The neoliberal subject's value is measured on the basis of its investment and productivity (Campbell, 2011: 73). From Mihic's (1980: 180) vantage, interpreting the right to die via human capital means that we must consider how:

> the supposedly autonomous dying patient is supposed to take into consideration the welfare of her or his loved ones. On the neoliberal human capital model, parents who love their children will try to close the self like a firm; they will try to die as efficiently as possible.

Those who age will not want to burden their loved ones; they would sooner die than become a dependent and interfere with the good, free, secured, immune person of their relatives.[3] Speaking from the vantage of the United States where health care is private and can leave families in serious debt, this concept of dependency as it relates to being a social burden has also become a central figure in assisted dying legal cases, particularly with response to economic considerations (Heasell and Paton, 2001).[4] One of the most recent comments from Daniel Callahan, a well-known speaker on aging and economics, even noted that we need to "let death have its day" given the burden that elderly persons cost to society in end of life care in our current socio-economic climate. Surely, then, the law is acting benevolently in denying assisted dying; it is simply protecting appellants from becoming an economic "solution" for a neoliberal society that would potentially benefit from fewer dependents (e.g., Callahan, 2008: 79–82; Humphrey, 1991).

As the intervener COPOH (Coalition of Provincial Organizations of the Handicapped) also observed:

> [t]he negative stereotypes and attitudes which exist about the lack of value and quality inherent in the life of a person with a disability are particularly dangerous in this context because they tend to support the conclusion that a suicide was carried out in response to those factors rather than because of pressure, coercion or duress.

We find the same discussion emerge in *Pretty v UK*, 2002, whereby the case drew on the work of the House of Lords Select Committee that had forced the point regarding "the undesirability of anything which could appear to encourage suicide" (House of Lords, 1994, paragraph 239). It stated as follows:

> We are also concerned that vulnerable people—the elderly, lonely, sick or distressed—would feel pressure, whether real or imagined, to request early death. We accept that, for the most part, requests resulting from such pressure or from remediable depressive illness would be identified as such by doctors and managed appropriately. Nevertheless we believe that the message which society sends to vulnerable and disadvantaged people should not, however obliquely, encourage them to seek death, but should assure them of our care and support in life.

This particular argument was also made in Fleming's (2013) case. The law argued that it was impossible to tell whether Fleming freely chose assisted death or whether she was coerced into it. The judge, Kearns, argued that because Fleming was a degenerate, and as such—because she was dependent on others—it would be impossible to detach her person from this dependent status: there would always be a possibility that she felt a "duty" to die. In short, a "death with dignity" would be a duty and responsibility for particular kinds of persons: those "dependents" who would burden others (Corlett, 2001; Sprung *et al.*, 1997); the law, it is claimed, is simply acting benevolently to protect us from this prospect: the law is protecting particular kinds of persons.

With these previous arguments in mind, this particular logic that law asserts suggests that: (a) anyone appealing for the right to die has possibly been coerced into this appeal on the basis that they have internalized social norms of what life counts and what life does not (thus they have appealed for their own subjection because of social pressure); and/or (b) if assisted dying were to be legalized those subjects deemed to be lacking a life worth living would inevitably be terminated or at least would face this possibility.

Law is not Benevolent: How Law Reinforces Social Norms

While the law might claim to act as a benevolent paternal force, arguably its discussions of assisted dying do not attend to the root of the problem, which is the relation that has been constructed in society between indignity and dependency. As noted already in this chapter, one of the central problems appears to be that subjects are fixed in particular ways as proper appellants for death. The person who ought to seek death is the person who is a dependent. The problem, therefore, is that certain persons are labeled as abject because they are dependents.[5] One finds support for this claim in the wording of legal cases on assisted dying. Law is only able to act "benevolently" with its problematic paternalism precisely because it plays a role in fixing subjects as dependents and as abject.

Categories of Persons in Assisted Dying Cases

As noted earlier, the constitution of types of person is invariably linked to the political rationality of governance (Rose, 1999). Different political rationalities will legitimate different distinctions between persons based on the values the rationality advances (Pavlich, 2013). For instance, in Pavlich's (2013) research on distinctions of persons at the Cape of Good Hope, governance under sovereignty politics rationalized a different distinction of persons to that of contemporary political rationalities. In our case, as noted earlier, in the contemporary society the abject person is the one who cannot conform to the neoliberal ethos of reciprocal independence: the abject person is the dependent person (Biggs and Powell, 2001; Phillipson, 1998; Powell, 2001; Townsend, 1981; Walker, 1982).

The law requires that it is possible to fix particular kinds of persons into categories because it renders these persons as the objects of law "visible and calculable" (Foucault, 1990a; Naffine, 2009; see also

Pavlich, 2013). Law can then act on subjects in a universalizing way given that their identities are constituted as fixed (Campbell, 2005). The constitution of the dependent subject—particularly *how one is framed as a dependent*—is a way of fixing subjects into a particular category. Dependency, as noted, is labeled negatively from a social perspective because it is not fitting with a neoliberal society that values relations of reciprocal independence whereby persons live privately and refrain from interfering with or obligating one another (Fine, 2005). Constituting subjects we deem as (or who claim to be) dependent fixes these people as abject.

Indeed, most scholars writing on assisted dying note that appellants and those who would be directly affected by legal reform regarding assisted dying fall into three "categories" or "types of person," as Esposito (2012a, 2012b) would note: those who experience a terminal illness; those who experience a disability; and those who are considered elderly, as noted above. Sometimes these categories are even used synonymously, which for some scholars such as those involved in critical disability studies poses its own set of challenges (Tremain, 2005). In each of these three identity categories, subjects are framed as "vulnerable" and degenerate on the basis that their "person" is articulated as being at a stage in life in which their life might be perceived by themselves and others as unqualified or not worth living precisely because it is dependent on others (Hiranandani, 2005).

In its response to assisted death, the law then claims to act as a benevolent sovereign force: it refuses assisted death claiming that one could not know whether an appellant seeking a death with dignity was instead coerced into this death. Because of the appellant's dependent, vulnerable personhood (universalized and fixed by law), the law cannot allow the prospect of assisted death and it generates the legal fiction of the immune person, as the subject requiring law's protection, and the immune society as the secure society (as noted in Chapter 4) that is also protected from havoc should the law not protect its vulnerable persons.

The association between an appeal to die and a duty to die does two things. First it relies on the abject status of the appellant to depersonalize their claim—their life is unqualified and dependent, so they cannot make a free decision; it would be impossible because their life is already bound with and to others. This legitimates the law's paternalism and the law's constitution of appellants as vulnerable, and it also legitimates the law's constitution of the other who would help assist death or support the appeal to death as an enemy, thus feeding the legal fiction of the immune person in an immune society who must be protected from outside interference. By fixing its object as a particular kind of person (a degenerate who is dependent), the law is able to reject the appellant's own assertion of sovereignty and its own immune person and immune society fiction whereby the appellant claims to protect loved ones from burden, in favor of a fiction of an immune society that protects appellants from themselves, and also that protects appellants from those they would otherwise trust. The law overrides the appeals with an assertion of its own legal fictions that claims to protect particular kinds of subjects.

This logic of law becomes even more apparent when we examine the wording of legal cases where appeals to death are denied due to claims that persons are not deemed degenerate "enough." Fixing subject positions and conforming to social norms about what life is worthy of death and what life is not based on this connection between the concept of dependency to indignity also allows the law to limit those who might seek death who do not conform to the proper subjectivity. Take for example the case of *Re E (Medical Treatment: Anorexia)* [2012] EWHC 1639 (COP). In the case of *Re E* the appellant, E, a 32-year-old woman, attempted to exercise her right to refuse treatment for anorexia nervosa. E was not appealing to an assisted death; she was simply committing what some might call a slow suicide through self-starvation. Yet arguably she was not the right kind of subject to die: though she was being supported in a hospice and was dependent on others and on machines, she was also a subject who could be potentially restored to health: her case was not "hopeless." Because she was not a proper subject in the sense that the court deemed she was not terminally ill, disabled or elderly, the law came up with a different rationale for making her live. Her case even cited a precedent in which the law had allowed a subject, Ms B, the right to refuse life sustaining treatment (a right that has been precedent since *Bland*) on the grounds that Ms B in *Ms B v An NHS Hospital Trust* [2002] EWHC 429 (Fam) had been paralyzed by a sudden illness and was left "dependent on mechanical ventilation and total nursing care." The case noted Ms B "chose to refuse continued life support despite retaining full mental abilities and having a substantial expectation of life. Her decision was upheld by the court, and she died." Despite discussing this case it did not set a precedent for E. That it did not set a precedent is telling: Ms B was a proper subject of death; E was not.

While the case of E might stir complaints because it is not a case on assisted death, arguably it is precisely because of this that it is telling for the narrative unfolding in this chapter regarding the concept of dependency. The law does not interfere in death when the subject, like Ms B, is dependent on others and on society such that he or she will never have a hope of regaining any independence and becoming "normal;" in contrast, E's case shows how law claims to protect some subjects by virtue of the prospect of being restored to this normal status. Returning to our assisted dying cases, the law does not claim that the appellants are not "proper" subjects: it does not refuse them an assisted death simply because dependency is, or ought to be, an acceptable social virtue and that we ought to, as a society, try to change the way we relate to one another. Rather, the law simply avoids the discussion of the norm of life that it takes for granted that labels some life worthy and other life unworthy as a matter of who is dependent and who can live independently; instead, as explained in Chapter 3 with reference to *Bland*, law focuses on the act of killing as that which would cause the alleged problem. In doing so it avoids the larger social problem and a discussion of social norms that places limits on what life counts and therefore also places limits on how we can relate to one another. We are simply to take for granted the "fact" that a dependent life that can never be restored to an independent life is an undignified one. Focusing on a difference between acts of killing conceals these underlying norms that allow such differentiations between acts to be made.

One could also call upon the instance in Belgium in 2013–2014 in which the Senate passed the controversial prospect that children might be able to seek assisted death: the prospect that children might desire their own death has caused much controversy, even if said children possibly fall into the "acceptable" categories of being terminally ill and/or disabled. Likewise, the case of the Belgium twins, Marc and Eddy Verbessen, elicited much media coverage due to the fact that they were born deaf and sought euthanasia together as they were becoming progressively blind. A number of media sources speculated whether they were "disabled enough;"[6] their case appeared to invoke less sympathy and popular support than appeals from subjects who seemingly fit the "appropriate" criteria to die such as appeals from frail, elderly persons or from those who are confined to a wheelchair. Caution with regard to this particular narrative that seeks to regulate assisted dying on the basis of being a "proper" subject of the right to die is therefore important.

The case of *Re E* also shows us not only how the appellants articulate their subject positions, but also how the law tends to fix these positions and reaffirm the prospect that certain subjects are suitable for death, while others are not. In the English and Canadian cases of assisted dying that were analyzed it became clear that the problem was not that the law deemed the subjects unsuitable for death (they were the right kind of subject—i.e. disabled, terminally ill); rather, the problem was that in most cases the law simply could not rationalize the act that would complete these subject's death because it would contradict its own legal fictions that were reflections of a neoliberal ethos.

One might object that the above claim is a bold one. How could one know that the law views the appellants as the "right kind of subjects" for assisted death? Likewise how could one know that the law denies the prospect of assisted death not on the basis of some appellants being the wrong kind of subject but instead because the act itself is not complicit with the legal fictions law projects? If one recalls the arguments put forth in Chapter 2 of this book one can note a defense to this claim. Chapter 2 showed how the law used the abject subjectivities of appellants in order to "fix" them as vulnerable subjects. The law claimed that they were vulnerable, even when they demanded that they were not (i.e. in the case of Nicklinson): the appellants in the cases examined were the right kind of subjects for assisted death, so much so that they need protecting from its very prospect. Indeed, this brings us full circle to the paradox that the appellants themselves are presented with: by fixing themselves as the right kind of subjects (i.e. claiming the right to die on the basis of their dependent status, which allowed the law to fix them as vulnerable—even if they then try and deny this subject position by working against it and claiming a personalization for themselves as discussed above), they have already fed the legal fiction of the immune person that allows law to deny them the prospect of assisted death.

While the law claims to be benevolent by protecting these dependents, instead, arguably, law helps create and reify the very problem: legal discussions and decisions on assisted dying continue to fix the appellants as particular kinds of people (elderly, disabled or terminally ill) who are all dependents and thereby undignified (i.e. persons who burden or obligate others). While the law might deny assisted death it does not challenge the social norms that allow indignity to get attached to dependency that construct particular kinds of subjects who are seeking assisted death as the proper subjects of such death. This means to suggest that the law does not challenge the social norms, such as the "fact" that certain kinds of people are legitimate in their appeals to death, which is shaped by the larger negative connotation of being a dependent in a society defined by an independent ethos; instead, the law simply, at present, shows a concern regarding the act of killing itself (i.e. how one gets rid of these dependents). It is this latter aspect of assisted dying appeals that does not comport with the overall legal fictions of the immune person and immune society and would thereby contradict the neoliberal ethos.

Neoliberal Law's Paradox of Assisted Dying

In short, and to bring this chapter to a close, the law's denial of assisted dying seems to be paradoxical: given that the law reflects the values of a neoliberal ethos, albeit by effect rather than design, much like Chapter 3 argued, it would seem logical to let abject subjects be killed via assisted death; it might feed a legal fiction of the neoliberal immune community that seeks to rid itself of dependents who interfere with the immune persons of those comprising the immune society. This is so given that what life counts or is "qualified" in the good neoliberal society is the life that can live independently and can contribute to the larger immune society by sustaining itself in a reciprocally independent relation with others.

However, this chapter like others has argued that one must look beyond the *ratio decidendi* and examine law as a discourse tied to the neoliberal rationality of governance. When one does this one finds that concepts emerge that feed legal fictions sustaining this rationality of governance. These legal fictions are both particularizing and universalizing and are based around a logic of protection of the bounded individual immune person who is part of a larger community of immune persons. The neoliberal ethos is one grounded in a desire to rid the immune society of burdens, yet it cannot do so in overt ways that would contradict its protective, particularizing logic. At base, while allowing the deaths of those deemed dependent might be beneficial to the neoliberal ethos, one could argue that the law simply has not yet found a way to rationalize some kinds of assisted deaths within this immunizing logic. Chapter 3 of this book also drew this conclusion through an analysis of the concept of inviolability of persons. Chapter 3 argued that the law made a differentiation between acts and omissions, or killing and letting die; it did so to rationalize some deaths through a logic of non-interference that could feed and sustain the legal fictions of immune persons and immune society complicit with a neoliberal ethos. This chapter on dependency has argued that those who are deemed more dependent are suitable subjects for assisted death, and those who can live independently are not. The law operates more and more as a norm, legitimating certain requests on the basis of their being at least the right kind of subject; however, in some instances refusing them because at present there is no "decent" moral way to dispose of these subjects that would not otherwise contradict the rationality itself. This ought to trouble us: if assisted death were to be rationalized, we ought to be concerned precisely how this rationalization would occur, particularly if it were in accordance with the reciprocally divisive ethos of neoliberalism (as Chapter 3 on *Bland*, for instance, highlighted).

Conclusion

This chapter has considered how the concept of dependency emerges in both appeals to assisted death and in legal decisions to deny assisted death. It has argued that the concept of dependency feeds the legal fictions of the immune person as a subject who desires a freedom from dependent relations, complicit with a larger neoliberal ethos that is grounded in an idea that the good society is the society in which all subjects are immune from one another, bound simply by their reciprocal non-interference with one another. The law operates as a discourse and as a technology of neoliberal political rationality that makes decisions in line with its political ethos that is progressively forging a society that relishes in individualism, non-interference and privatization. A neoliberal ethos supports and encourages relations between subjects that are increasingly immune from one another. The chapter has also argued that the law claims to act as a benevolent sovereign in its protection of subjects from this neoliberal ethos: it claims to protect subjects from the internalization of social norms that render some lives less valuable than others on the basis of their being more dependent. Law claims to deny assisted death in order to protect vulnerable subjects, much like Chapter 2 argued, from the "slippery slope" that would lead to vulnerable subjects being killed by those who deem them a burden. The law thus feeds a legal fiction of an immune person whom it protects from outside interference.

The chapter also argued that, while law appears to act benevolently, it actually instead serves to fix subject positions and uses these fixed subject positions to continue to deny assisted death in some instances. Law does not challenge social norms that construct certain persons (e.g., elderly, disabled, terminally ill) as dependents and therefore as the proper appellants for assisted death; instead law fixes these subjects as the right kind of subjects for assisted death and therefore as inevitably vulnerable to outside interference. This is a problem because the law does not then challenge the idea that some lives are more worthy than others, but rather confirms this idea and then claims to protect unworthy life from the interference of outsiders based on its legal fictions. Recalling Chapter 3 that considered the concept of inviolability, this lack of deconstruction of social norms that fix subjects as particular kinds of persons ought to concern us; Chapter 3 showed us how the law is able to differentiate between kinds of lives that it deems worthy and unworthy by creating distinctions of "acts," some of which are not deemed complicit with its fiction of the immune person (active killing), and some of which are said to be complicit (such as withdrawal of care). The law seems to operate as a norm; it does not overtly make distinctions between qualified and unqualified life so much as it instead makes these distinctions more subtly with reference to a concept of inviolability shared by all, that can be used to rationalize the death of some it deems unqualified and not others. The law reflects the ethos of neoliberalism because it maintains the legal fictions of immune persons and immune society that such an ethos requires. Because the law operates as a norm that reflects a neoliberal ethos, this means to suggest that the law might not have yet found ways to get rid of some of its dependent subjects like those appealing for assisted death in ways that conform to the neoliberal ethos, but this does not mean such a prospect might not be possible in the future. Indeed, while it is still early days for Canadian law, the recent decision on Taylor's case in *Carter v Canada* (2015) highlights this potential.

My intent here is not to claim that assisted dying as a practice is necessarily good nor bad *per se*; rather, the intent is to show the ways that the law's decisions on this practice reflect wider power knowledge relations that are deeply bound to a particularizing and universalizing logic based on the reciprocal protection of individual life. At present, legal decisions that deny assisted dying do nothing to challenge what appears to be the core problem which, as this chapter has argued, is that society does not value relations of dependency. Devaluing relations of dependency means that particular subjects who might be regarded as interfering with the freedom of others by way of being a dependent on these others can be constructed as a vulnerable subject and the right kind of subject for assisted death. It also means conversely that if one does not conform to being this particular kind of person one is alternatively not the right kind of subject for assisted death, which, as the chapter has argued, is constraining for others who might seek death.

The argument advanced is that if a neoliberal ethos is one that attempts to completely immunize us from relations of dependence, a more "affirmative" political ethos would open itself up to the prospect that dependent relations are not only necessary but are also inevitable: while we require the protection of individual life to some degree, it seems that in the current era this protection of life has gone too far and risks falling into the very opposite: a destructive power that in its alleged protection actually risks this life (Esposito, 2008, 2011). Indeed if one looks at the very concept of assisted dying, where persons are seeking a death that is independent, they are also seeking this independence with the help of another. The sovereign death being sought is not sovereign after all. Likewise, as noted in previous chapters, even a would-be sovereign death such as suicide would inevitably implicate others. As the House of Lords Select Committee noted in 1994 (paragraph 237), cited in *Pretty v UK*: "dying is not only a personal or individual affair. The death of a person affects the lives of others, often in ways and to an extent which cannot be foreseen." All death leaves an imprint on those around one's self; no death is entirely individual and independent. To aim for such an independent death is to strive for the completion of a fiction that is simply that: fictive. The wording of assisted dying legal appeals and the concepts law draws on to feed legal fictions that reflect a neoliberal, immunizing ethos reveals this problematic paternalism; it also reveals how this paternalism closes us off to other kinds of relations that the ethos of neoliberalism does not encourage or permit.

What follows in the concluding chapter is not only a summary of the key arguments presented throughout this book but also a gesture toward how a different politics of assisted death might be imagined: how might one challenge the social norms that regard dependency in a negative light, and how might one ensure that appeals themselves and the laws that deny them consider assisted death in ways that perhaps undo the legal fictions of immune person and immune society that the previous chapters of the book have argued are fed through various concepts that close subjects off from one another?

Notes

1 The colloquial phrase has become part of the widespread liberal battle against current law that precludes this legal right to die. One of the earliest uses of this phrase amidst the right to die debates was found in Oregon's Death With Dignity Act passed in 1997. The phrase has since made its way into Canada's Bill C-384, which encompassed the concept, entitled: *An Act to Amend the Criminal Code (right to die with dignity)*, 2nd Sess., 40th Parl., introduced in the House of Commons in May 2009. Quebec's *Dying with Dignity Report* in 2012 has been followed by its most recent Bill 52, tabled in June 2013, *An Act Respecting End of Life Care*, which also notes in its first line that the purpose of the bill is to

ensure end of life care that is "respectful of ... dignity and ... autonomy and to recognize the primacy of wishes expressed freely and clearly with respect to end-of-life care." Moreover, it might be no surprise that Switzerland's national euthanasia clinic is termed "Dignitas," the term from which dignity is a derivative.

2 From a definitional and etymological standpoint, the term dignity is most broadly akin to honor and respect. In Latin it translates as *amplitudo*, denoting greatness and grandeur, and as noted above it is a derivative of the Roman word *dignitas*, meaning "authority" or "charisma." Indeed this seems to be how we arrive at the word dignitary, meaning someone of rank. Thomas Hobbes had a similar conception of dignity, which he equated with power. For him, dignity was something personal and it indicated that one had value. Someone with charisma, who could persuade persons of his or her worth, had dignity. This reference to charisma is particularly interesting when considering Esposito's genealogy of the dispositif of the person, whereby he describes the charisma of the person as "a gift" (2012b: 22). In his essay *Enough of Self*, Campbell also speaks to this concept whereby he notes that this term charisma derives from the Greek Kharisma, meaning a divine "gift of grace" (2012: 38). For Max Weber, too, charisma is considered that which separates particular individuals from ordinary persons. Campbell suggests that this uptake of Kharisma is biopolitically important, particularly when considered as a secularized concept in a neoliberal era. He posits: "The first layer of thanatopolitics in contemporary biopower will be found in the separation that the dispositif enacts over man and in particular in separating what properly and improperly belongs to him as a person thanks to neoliberalism's appropriation of grace" (2012: 39). What is particularly interesting about Campbell's note regarding charisma is its link to grace and to the constitution of the proper subject.

3 One might also, however, consider on the basis of human capital, that individuals as Campbell (2011: 73) suggests "harvest their own biopower" —the governance of the self under neoliberalism somewhat maps onto the ethics of self-care that Foucault imagined. While Campbell is cautious that an ethics or affirmative bio-politics does not "do the bidding of neoliberalism" we might imagine that Foucault's later work was an attempt to think about how an ethics of self-care might evolve out of the contemporary rationality of governance that treats said subjects as human capital whereby their value is based on their productivity as individuals. Or, at the very least, an affirmative politics must bear this in mind and consider a relational way of constituting an ethics of the self from within the very social conditions one finds oneself. It would be paralyzing to think that we could not do "anything" because any movement would result in a claim of mere subjection.

4 See, for example, the Nancy Cruzan case. Economic cost is not discussed in English, Canadian or Irish legal appeals.

5 One can note here that one is speaking to dependents who are thus conceived as "irreversibly" so. This differentiates dependents who have the alleged potential to become independent (e.g. children, or as with the case of *Re E* [2012] discussed later in the book).

6 See, for example, CBC News article: www.cbc.ca/news/world/death-of-twin-brothers-fuels-debate-over-belgian-euthanasia-law-1.133486

Conclusion

Three Theses for an Affirmative Politics of Assisted Death

The opening pages of this book described the problem of assisted dying as a problem of community: our current political rationality of neoliberalism emphasizes relations between subjects that are privative, independent and divisive. Neoliberal subjects are encouraged to seek a life that is free from obligation toward others and from others; neoliberal subjects are immunized subjects (Esposito, 2008, 2011). It has been argued throughout that the law operates as a discourse and technology of this neoliberal governance. An analysis of assisted dying legal cases from England and Canada, two western neoliberal counties, reveals this point. The background work to this book involved an extensive exegesis of these cases and also drew on cases from the United States and Ireland as supporting evidence. It involved the examination of various political texts, parliamentary bills and task force documents that have contributed to the building of the larger picture regarding how the law currently treats assisted dying—ranging from practices of palliative sedation, passive euthanasia, physician assisted death to voluntary active euthanasia.

When examining the wording of legal cases on assisted dying in the context of its wider power-knowledge relations the book has argued that assisted dying laws, by effect rather than by design, reflect this larger neoliberal ethos: the discussions and decisions made in case law reflect a divisive, privatizing rationality. While focusing on law's decisions, this book has also considered how appellants express their appeals to assisted death. In particular, it has been argued that these appeals themselves reflect a larger neoliberal ethos: appellants, for instance, articulated desires for personal security; some like Nicklinson denied vulnerability; others like Rodriguez claimed to be rational and autonomous, able to make decisions free from the coercion of others; and subjects articulated a desire to be free from relations that they argued rendered them dependent on others. Both the law that denied assisted death and the appellants who sought it framed their positions within this divisive, closed and privative logic.

My interest in the question and prospect of community and my concern regarding how law operates as a mechanism that seems to reinforce neoliberal dissociations from community led me to focus on the pastoral logic underpinning legal cases. The book has focused on how legal cases have developed concepts, as noted above, which feed legal fictions that overlap with the pastoral mode of governance directed at the one and the many, or the particular and the universal. It has been noted, drawing on Foucault (2003), that a neoliberal ethos emphasizes increasingly closed off and privative subjectivities shaped in accordance with the governance of the whole community. The preceding chapters have shown, in various ways, how legal decisions drew on various concepts that fed legal fictions, reflecting the individualizing and totalizing tendencies of the neoliberal rationality. Chapter 2 emphasized the concepts of enmity and vulnerability; Chapter 3 examined the concept of inviolability; Chapter 4 considered the concept of security; and Chapter 5 discussed the concept of dependency. Each chapter argued that the concepts expressed in legal cases fed the two interrelated legal fictions of the "immune person" and the "immune society." An analysis revealed how the fiction of the immune person reflected the particularizing tendency of neoliberalism that sought to maintain borders around particular subjects who were to be divided from one another; it also revealed how the fiction of the immune society reflected the universalizing feature of neoliberalism, which emphasized a totality of reciprocally dissociated persons. It has been argued that the "ideal" neoliberal society, if brought to fruition, would be a society in which subjects are as closed off as much as they can possibly be from one another such that subjects can live with as much freedom from interference and from obligation as possible. This was called, following Oliva (2006), the reciprocally dissociative society. The legal fiction of the former immune person was constructed in assisted dying legal cases through various concepts (e.g., enmity, vulnerability, inviolability, security and dependency) in order to present the idea that individuals are private, sovereign, independent selves who are dissociated from others. The legal fiction of the latter immune society was constructed simultaneously as a totality of immune persons that sometimes required protecting from the immune persons themselves who might otherwise threaten the totality (e.g. in the case of security, liberty, enmity and dependency).

Together the chapters indicated how legal fictions emerge from a neoliberal politics. However, it was also noted from the onset that law is not simply a conduit of this politics; rather, law is socially shaped and has the potential to create a new kind of politics. "Law is dependent on the powers that exist outside it and … these powers are themselves dependent upon the law," write Golder and Fitzpatrick (2009: 71). Law is mutable and responsive. Where this book shows how the law through appeals to the "right to die" operates as a mutable conduit for a neoliberal ethos, this concluding chapter turns to the potential responsiveness of law. Drawing from and summarizing the main points raised throughout the book, it alludes to the possibility of articulating an "affirmative" politics of assisted dying. Three key theses can be drawn from the previous analysis to help devise such an affirmative politics of assisted death.

What is an Affirmative Politics?

My image of an affirmative politics is indebted to Esposito's (2008) insights that not only highlight the link between immunizing forms of life and the prospect of community but that also point to a more optimistic kind of politics that can be sought. If the problem with law's treatment of assisted dying legal cases is that it enforces a paternalistic politics that excessively immunizes individuals from one another, then an affirmative politics would consider ways that such a politics could reverse mechanisms of immunization toward the openness that the prospect of community might yield. Esposito calls this, contra to a personal politics, or a proper politics, an "impersonal" one. An impersonal politics conceptualizes relationality as that which constitutes us *a priori* such that our being in relation is what makes it possible for us to forge space for ourselves: "being" as a singular (and not individual) subject is thus only possible on the basis of the ontological "with" (Nancy, 2000). This seems to be precisely the point that Esposito speaks about with regard to community and the originary *munus*. Indeed, when Esposito speaks of the "improper community" and "impersonal," which is a "community of nothing" and a community of "non-persons" that he gestures toward in his affirmative politics, he refers to the gap or spacing as the being-in-common:

> This means that we should identify at least two meanings, or levels, of the nothing, which must be kept separate in spite of and within their apparent coincidence. While the first level is, as we have seen, that of a relationship—the gap, or the spacing, that makes the being-in-common a relation, not an entity—the second is, on the

> other hand, that of its dissolution: the dissolution of the relationship in the absoluteness of the without-relation.[1]

One might note as per Esposito that the immune individual can only be understood in relation to the community, and the community in relation to the *munus*. This is to suggest that any mechanism of immunization is never complete, but rather is always tied to the originary *munus* that is a relational way of being to which the subject can be re-exposed by "bringing the outside in" that inevitably occurs with any and all processes of immunization (such is the "nature" of biological immunity itself). As Jean Luc Nancy warns, one must not confuse this relationality with "a revival of a certain Christian and humanistic emphasis on 'sharing,' 'exchange,' or 'others'" (in Lopez, 2013: 21). Rather, in being-with, in the *munus*, what we share is a void, or the "spacing" that provides the very possibly of being (Lopez, 2013). The community "isn't the *inter* of *esse* but rather *esse* as *inter*, not a relationship that shapes being [*essere*] but being itself as the relation" (Esposito, 2010: 139).

Yet, from Esposito's perspective, the exposure to the *munus* is dangerous and is what drives immunity. This being-in-common that is relationally constituted is a state that is always both one of contagion and relation. Exposure to the *munus* is always that which places us at risk because the *munus* expropriates; it takes us outside of ourselves. And this is precisely the meaning of existence itself—it is the exposure to the outside that we find in an originary relational *munus*. It is under immunity mechanisms that we are protected from this exposure, but to the point that "one is deprived of the exposure that is existence itself" (Lopez, 2013: 21). "Immunity ... is necessary to the preservation of individual and collective life—since no one would be alive without an immune system" notes Esposito (2012c); however, it is when immunity takes on "an exclusive and excluding shape with respect to any environmental and human otherness" that it ends up stifling the very "development of life itself."

Esposito's version of an affirmative bio-politics intends to reverse the immunitarian drive. He imagines an affirmative bio-politics in which immunity holds within it a contagion, such that the process of immunization is always opening and shifting rather than static. If a dangerous politics endeavors to remove all contagion by immunizing the self from the other then an affirmative politics instead considers how contagion can relate us to one another. He describes this as a relational-contagious experience (Esposito, 2013: 85; Lemm, 2012). This is the point that Esposito raises in his account of common immunity.

Common Immunity

In *Immunitas*, Esposito puts forth the notion of a "common immunity" that opens up the possibility of an affirmative bio-politics, or an opening of the self to the other. One can note here that Esposito states two readings of biological immunization. The first is configured on account of the idea of immunity operating as a military device that rationalizes the "violent defense in the face of anything judged to be foreign" (Esposito, 2011: 17). Yet the second account of immunization offers "another interpretive possibility" that situates it in association with community and openness such that "once its negative power has been removed, the immune is not the enemy of the common but rather something more complex that implicates and stimulates the common" (2011: 18). The first reading is a misinterpretation of how immunity operates. It is within the latter reading of immunization that notes the indissociable relation between immunity and community that reveals the space for an affirmative politics, one in which recognition of the other—not necessarily the other that one "knows" or who is made known as a private other like Arendt had warned but the other who is a stranger to us—as part of our constitutive makeup can take over "from the lexicon of war" (Esposito, 2011: 165–166).

A particular example Esposito draws on to illustrate this affirmative reading of immunization is that of pregnancy. He explains how the survival of the fetus is only made possible by virtue of the fact that the fetus, which takes on genetic foreignness from the father, is protected by the mother's secretion of antibodies that work to conceal the fetus's "foreign" state. He asks: "How can the fetus, encoded as 'other' based on all normal immunological criteria, be tolerated by the maternal antibodies? ... Women develop certain types of antibodies permitting the embryo to survive by hiding the signals it secretes indicating that it is foreign" (2011: 169). Following this, he notes that "by immunizing the other, it is also immunizing itself. It immunizes itself from an excess of immunization ... antibodies are still what block or 'fool' the self-defense system of the mother" (2011: 169). In this description of pregnancy Esposito manages to shift the immunitary horizon not from that which grants the proper to what is same, but to that which grants the proper to the stranger, or other (see also O'Byrne, 2013). Esposito's thesis suggests that through birth something complex happens within the immune condition such that it is not sameness that protects the fetus and the mother from one another but it is their very difference that allows the child to be born. He writes: "Only as a stranger can the child become proper" (2011: 170). One might read this here as a disruption of the idea of who can count as proper and who cannot; through difference we can recognize the proper of others.

The analogy of the common immunity in pregnancy is a useful heuristic device to consider a more important point specifically pertaining to the association of difference with what is proper, which is to challenge the common association of the proper with sameness or heterogeneity (see also Derrida, 2000). In affirming the stranger or other as proper—or perhaps better, by not affirming those who are the same as us or known to us as the only subjects who are proper—one can begin to shift from what Esposito calls norms over life to norms of life whereby difference emerges. For example, from the vantage of community or the neoliberal political ideas about what life counts as good and proper, it would mean opening up this idea to generate different norms of life (Esposito, 2008). As Esposito (2008: 190) suggests: "Once again it is the "norm of life" that is in play, but according to an order that, rather than circumscribing life within the limits of the norm, opens the norm to the infinite unpredictability of life." The "maximum deconstruction" of the immunitary paradigm rests precisely on the prospect of creating "continually new norms" (Esposito, 2008: 190).

Third Person Politics

One can also consider here what Esposito calls his impersonal politics, or a politics of the third person. This might help us think about a different way to conceive of relationality that breaks down normative discourses regarding the good life and opens up the prospect of creating multiple, new norms. Esposito explains that the third person differs to the first person that refers to the pronunciation of "I" that divides one from another and the second person, "you," which, like the first, is reversibly also an "I" in relation to oneself (2012a: 105). "As much as the I may want to respect the you in its independence, preserving it in its transcendence, the I cannot help but exert an effect of mastery over it, since that alterity is logically dependent on the definition of the I itself," says Esposito (2012a: 105–106). The "you" can therefore never be anything but a non-I and vice versa because "only one can occupy it—the one who calls itself I—the subjectivization of the first term automatically desubjectifies the second, until such time as it acquires subjectivity in its turn by desubjectifying the first" (2012a: 106). Esposito's point is to suggest that personhood as well as law relies on divisions between subjects—the former relies on a division between the subject himself or herself such that he or she is personalized by controlling the animal part; the latter relies on divisions between subjects some who can occupy a place of the first person "I" but only on account of making others a second person (you) and de-subjectifying them. An affirmative bio-politics cannot, therefore, rely on this division that the dispositif necessarily maintains between I and you, self and other.

Breaking down these binaries pushes one to consider how an impersonal datum must recognize how "I" and "you" are constituted by the same shared being-in-relation. This is what Esposito calls the third person, which he understands as the absence of the subjective quality or the idea of personal identity. As he writes, "the only person that has a plural, even when it is in the singular—or rather, precisely because it is in the singular—is the third" – because it is a non-person and it is neither singular nor plural but both" (2012a: 108). When Esposito (2012a: 108–109) says that the third person is a "non-person," what he seems to suggest is that to be in the third person or to act in the third person is to multiply the norm of life in such a way that it breaks down binaries between what is normal/abnormal, who is personalized/depersonalized. Where technologies of governance like law divides subjects between the animal part and human part, the abnormal/degenerate and normal, those who are immune and those who are not, the multiplication of norms of life would break down such that all life would be respected in its singularity as life itself. It is these key aspects of Esposito's affirmative bio-politics that I draw on here.

Three Theses

As should now be evident, this book has examined law as a discourse and technology of governance that enunciates legal fictions driven by a political rationality demanding increasing immunization. As noted before, in exploring the pastoral logic underpinning assisted dying case law, the book has examined how law closes subjects off from one another in ways that are both particularizing and totalizing. Law as a discourse and technology of neoliberalism presents a problematic paternalism over subjects that claims to protect individual legal subjects whilst at the same time dividing all subjects from one another in line with a pastoral logic of unity grounded in division.

In contrast, an affirmative politics highlights three key points that will be stated plainly before being elaborating upon. Throughout, the book has argued that legal practices around assisted dying, at present, comply with social norms. Thus, the first point of call for an affirmative politics is to act as a practice of critique of these norms. In this instance, case law would shift from being a conduit of social norms toward a practice of critique through the construction of case law as a space of dialogue and critical thought, that will manifest in a more innovative use of precedent to reshape the existing limiting social norms. Second, it will be concluded that, at present, the law and appeals themselves serve to fix subjects in a personal, privatized logic; in contrast, an affirmative politics will find and create ways to treats subjects within cases, and also treats the cases themselves, as relationally constituted and thereby never fixed or knowable. Case law will become a space that does not replace norms with new ones but will seek to revalue and proliferate norms. Learning from the conclusions drawn in this book, this affirmative space of law will not only arise through new precedent, but also will arise through the refusal to fix subjects (appellants, as well as those would assist with death) as certain kinds of subjects. Finally, where the pages of this book have shown how case law on assisted dying currently closes law off to change, an affirmative politics would treat law as continually open and responsive: the creation of new precedent on assisted death, and the multiplication of possible subjectivities within this space, would ask and require that that law remain open to new prospects. Like processes of immunization and communization, law is never complete but is always creating new ways of being in the world. What follows is a closer look at these "three theses" on an affirmative politics of assisted death.

Thesis One: The Responsiveness of Law or Law as Critique

One might argue that the book has thus far presented a rather passive view of law. Arguably, the analysis supported this passive reading: the wording of legal cases and the ways that these cases drew on concepts to feed legal fictions that were enunciations of a neoliberal ethos demonstrated that for the most part the law has done little to challenge the social norms that undergird the legal cases and feed the legal decisions. The various chapters of the book also made it clear how the law operates as a social norm rather than as a practice of critique. Chapter 2 argued that the law invoked concepts of vulnerability and enmity in ways that also did not challenge the norms that underpinned assisted dying requests. The law instead served to fix particular kinds of persons—those who are dependents and are therefore articulated as hopeless by societies' standards—as "vulnerable persons." Like

Chapters 2 and 5 noted, fixing subjects as vulnerable and fixing other subjects as enemies who would naturally want to kill these vulnerable subjects should they have the opportunity did not deconstruct the social norms that, in the first instance, labeled these persons as vulnerable. The law did not critique the norm; instead the law claimed to act as a benevolent sovereign power that would protect fixed abject persons, bringing the norm into being in law.

Chapter 3, likewise, noted the same effect: the law ignored how norms of life underscored what life was seen to count as qualified and what life was deemed simply abject; instead it found a way to let the latter abject subjects die through its differentiation between acts and omissions. The law did not challenge the idea that Bland's life, for instance, was of no value; nor did it challenge the idea that other appellants like Rodriguez's were of less value. It did not critique the social norm. Rather, it encompassed the norm within its decision when it allowed Bland's abject life to end in accordance with the larger neoliberal ethos of non-interference. The decision in *Bland* did not challenge the logic of non-interference, nor did it critique the prospect that the law was only deciding on Bland's life precisely because society's norms had declared it abject. Instead law concealed this norm in a decision to universalize all subjects under the alleged protection of law; law protected a social norm of non-interference even though this social norm was divisive.

Finally, Chapter 4 on security showed how the law differentiated between positive obligations and liberty interests which allowed it to reinforce the "fact" that the good, normal society operates best when persons do not interfere with one another; when appellants claimed the right to security of their person, case law claimed that it operated for the good of society and was under no obligation to protect positive rights and freedoms that might interfere with the freedoms and rights of others. The cases suggest a distinction between a negative obligation to protect persons from non-interference, complicit with the neoliberal ethos of reciprocal dissociation, and a positive obligation that would require that law take steps to intervene in persons' lives that it argued did not comport with its logic.

Drawing attention to the concepts that emerge in legal cases on assisted dying and how these concepts feed legal fictions to enunciate a neoliberal ethos allows one to note how the law might operate differently. This book had indicated how legal fictions, *as fictions*, are not immutable truths; they are instead reflective of wider power-knowledge relations. Law operates as a particular discourse and technology in which these power-knowledge relations are realized. One of the earlier scholars on legal fictions, Bentham, had said that we ought to "demystify" law's fictions. As a discourse and political technology, law does not simply create fictions independently of social norms: these are not simply law's fictions, but rather they are socio-legal fictions because they feed an ethos that exists outside of law and that in turn permeates law. It has also been argued that law is not simply a conduit of these socio-legal fictions but has the potential to reshape the fictions through changes in the operation of law. Given this, an affirmative politics of assisted dying ought to demystify, through law, socio-legal fictions. As a practice of critique the law would consider, following Pavlich (2001)—drawing on Foucault (1997)—how it might perpetually seek ways of "how not to be governed thus."

Expectations of Law

One might suggest that one ought not blame law for its passivity. Why should one expect law to deconstruct social norms? At least at present one might argue that law is a product of neoliberalism and creates legal fictions on the basis of this rationality: it unwittingly—that is, by effect rather than design—creates a neoliberal ethos through its concepts and legal fictions. In short, law is not divorced from the social norms it brings into being (Golder and Fitzpatrick, 2009). Despite the current passivity of law, this does not mean that law cannot take on a more critical role: law might indeed be a conduit of a political rationality, but law can also become a space for critique (Golder and Fitzpatrick, 2009). Law, and especially case law that is judge-made and spends time covering various positions on subject matter from witness statements, so-called "experts," and even scholarly work on the topic, can provide a productive space to hold discussions about social norms (Valverde, 2003). Were law to be understood as a practice of social critique it could potentially deconstruct social norms (Golder and Fizpatrick, 2009). Likewise, the association between law and immunity is also not strictly inhibiting: one could argue that Esposito's thesis provides a way of conceiving law not simply as that which is inhibiting and constrained to protecting that which is "proper," but rather that law can be thought "outside of the immunitary grip," as Amendola states (2012: 113). This then forms the first part of my affirmative politics: case law must become a practice of critique that plays an active role in deconstructing the social norms that bring appeals to bear and currently frame legal discussions and decisions. Cases would not make decisions on the basis of a *ratio decidendi* but rather would consider appeals within the context of power-knowledge relations. For instance, the various chapters have shown how, in the main, the law currently misses the opportunity to critique social norms. Instead, the chapters have shown how the law reinforces these norms through concepts and fictions that sustain a neoliberal ethos. This ethos is one that posits the good society as the reciprocally dissociative society.

Challenging Social Norms

By virtue of its method, this book has already demonstrated the type of critique that law might take on board. Chapter 5 most readily emphasized law's failure to challenge social norms that underpin assisted dying cases. The principle problem underpinning the question of assisted dying was the neoliberal ethos that perpetuated a social norm of independent, reciprocally dissociative relations between persons. Because of this social norm, subjects come to associate forms of dependency as degeneracy: being elderly, ill or disabled is to be degenerate because one is a dependent and places obligations onto others who, by virtue of the neoliberal ethos, are encouraged to value a freedom from dependent relations. An analysis of assisted dying cases revealed that the law did not challenge these social norms that attached dependency to degeneracy but instead reinforced them through the creation of legal fictions of the immune person and immune society. These fictions allowed the law to reinforce social norms and emphasize how practices of assisted death would not comport with the norm of reciprocal dissociation. It also reinforced these norms when it did not challenge their basic assumptions about what life was worth living and what life was not worth living but instead simply confirmed the "fact" that some lives are dependent and hopeless, while others have the prospect of being independent and therefore are not hopeless.

Innovations in Precedent

Second, in examining cases as playing into wider power-knowledge regimes, case law would not simply apply existing precedent as it currently does. Currently, precedent will be drawn on in an "act of judgment" to apply a universal principle to a particular case (Baxter, 2012: 162), which then in turn legitimates law's use of concepts and fictions to rationalize and reinforce the tenets of this existing law. Conversely, critical case law would instead use the prospect of precedent to become a practice of critique (Lefebvre, 2005, 2008). Rather than allowing precedent to fix case law that is imposed on subjects or creates and constructs subjects through fictions, one could argue that precedent poses a potential space for case law to be opened and extended. If *stare decisis* means to "stand by things decided," as Lefebvre (2008: 171) writes, one could argue that "the same points never occur exactly in litigation." For example, the assisted dying case of Gloria Taylor highlighted that Justice Lynn Smith and Chief Justice Beverley McLachlin were open to the prospect that the alleged precedent set in *Rodriguez* was not binding because it did not apply to Taylor's case. Justices Smith and McLachlin arguably, in Taylor's case, began to demonstrate a more affirmative approach to assisted dying law: Smith's extensive case opened space for dialogue; she did not simply close the case with *Rodriguez* as *stare decisis* but rather challenged this case. She showed how law might respond more openly. McLachlin did the same. While Smith's decision to allow Taylor a constitutional exemption and McLachlin's decision to stand by Smith certainly presented a closure of sorts through the act of making a legal decision, this new treatment of Taylor's case arguably worked to proliferate the norms of assisted dying laws: both Justices made possible a new affirmative space for the prospect of assisted death that had not previously existed. As it was recognized in the most recent 2015 *Carter v Canada* judgment, Smith's decision to move beyond *Rodriguez* and set a new precedent should not have been condemned so quickly. While *stare decisis* is viewed as a "constitutional principle" and is deemed necessary for the possible universal application of a legal system that allows "certainty while permitting the orderly development of incremental steps," as McLachlin (paragraph 43–44) noted, *stare decisis* "is not a strait jacket that condemns the law to stasis."

Treating cases on an individual basis and allowing law to make decisions that are not bound by existing precedent but rather to make decisions based on the particularities of the case means that law can create more and more precedents: it means that law can multiply precedents. Arguably this is an example of an affirmative politics that could be used in instances of assisted dying. Thinking about law as a practice of critique that treats legal cases as particularities would allow law to innovate around questions of assisted dying rather than being bound to previous decisions (Lefebvre, 2005, 2008). This would multiply the prospects for the directions the law might take. While Esposito (2008, 2013) does not speak directly to law in his affirmative bio-politics, he does speak to the multiplication of norms as part of this politics, which he calls more broadly a third person politics. Moreover, such an approach is fitting with Esposito's Deleuzian-inspired work in which Deleuze has praised the notion of jurisprudence that acquires its principles from the singularity of cases. Such an approach does not try to move outside of the sphere of law itself, but rather works immanently from within law to consider how law may become a space which can proliferate norms of life, rather than applying a norm of life through law. As Amendola (2012: 116) writes, such an approach can enable us to

> pass from the critique of law in so far as it is an immunitary apparatus ... to the construction of a law of the living capable of identifying, within the very same juridical norm ... a positive potentiality capable of moving beyond the lexicon of simple immunitarian normalization: a law that does not homologize or neutralize, but instead incorporates and defends that infinite production of difference and singularity.

Arguably the proliferation of legal norms through the instances in which more and more precedents are established from the particularities of each case is one example of such a third person politics that I now turn to in more detail.

Second Thesis: Law as a Third Person Politics

As noted previously, the first person politics refers to the pronunciation of "I" that divides one from another; likewise, the second person, "you," like the first person, is reversibly also an "I" in relation to oneself (Esposito, 2012a: 105). A politics that is critical of the first and second person notes how appeals to death and the law that denies them in accordance with social norms of life currently relies on divisions between subjects. An affirmative politics, practiced through law as critique, cannot rely on this division between I and you, self and other.

A Critique of "Rights"

Law as a third person politics breaks down these binaries between self and other that is shored up through "rights" appeals which assert and feed a legal fiction of an immune person divided from other immune persons. To break down these binaries between self and other that are embedded in a neoliberal ethos and therefore currently embedded in legal rights appeals as well as legal discussions and judgments, Esposito argues that a third person politics must recognize how the same shared being-in-relation constitutes "I" and "you:" the third person is the absence of the subjective quality or the idea of personal identity. As he writes, "the only person that has a plural, even when it is in the singular—or rather, precisely because it is in the singular—is the third"—because it is a non-person and it is neither singular nor plural but both (2012a: 108).

A critique of rights is important in order to heed Campbell's (2011, 2012) warning that an affirmative politics must not do the "dirty work" of neoliberalism. Campbell and others such as McNay (2009) caution us against advocating in favor of "rights" based appeals such as the "right to die;" they argue that such rights appeals which claim autonomy of the individual to self-direction over the body have a tendency to reproduce the neoliberal imperative to stake ownership of, and responsibility over, one's body. As McNay notes (2009: 64), these neoliberal practices reorient social relations around enterprise and are highly contentious: "The orchestration of individual existence as enterprise atomizes our understanding of social relations, eroding collective values and intersubjective bonds of duty and care at all levels of society."

Campbell (2013) is also particularly skeptical and critical of what he calls a "neoliberal entrepreneurship of the self." Similar to McNay, he notes the potential for this type of self-stylization to replicate insidious neoliberal tendencies of autonomy, individual agency, self-responsibility and immunizing closure. Therefore it is suggested that a cautious approach is taken when advocating for an individual's "rights" and "free choice" that also considers how these rights and freedoms are attached to broader governmental norms of life that have pronounced these lives as not worth living, and how these norms may have subsequently been internalized by subjects and used to develop immunizing closures around subjects (Campbell, 2011, 2012). In many ways this corresponds with the suggestions of scholars like Paul Patton who note the need for a non-transcendent, immanent conception of rights. For Patton (2012), as well as Hanafin (2007) who applies his work to the Italian laws on reproductive rights, one must not do away with rights but reconceive of them to recognize their materiality. For Hanafin, this is the case of the "biological citizen," which advocates for a jurisprudence that is created by vital subjects resisting a sovereign imposed law and opening up this law to new ways of being. Yet as noted previously, one must be careful in how one articulates such a conception. The affirmative politics expressed here then claims that law must work from singularities and let the singularities of cases drive the norm rather than vice versa. However, one must also consider the ways that individual subjectivities of appellants are already shaped by larger social norms, particularly immunizing ones. Where Hanafin (2014: 107) for instance writes that "individuals take responsibility for their selves and work on the political and legal terrains to being about real change," Campbell warns that we must ensure that such change does not simply do the bidding of neoliberalism. To what extent is individual responsibility not only a neoliberal subjectivity but also one that perpetuates neoliberal, proper immunized forms of life? Decisions to die may be based on a socio-political logic that subjects internalize, not wanting burden others; not wanting to appear vulnerable. Does this mean we should simply heed their appeals as an example of a "vital" politics of life that is simply resistive?

Breaking down Binaries

To be in the third person or to act in the third person is to multiply the norm of life in such a way that it breaks down binaries between what is normal/abnormal, who is personalized/depersonalized. Where legal decisions as well as rights appeals themselves currently reinforce divisions within subjects between the animal part and human part, and between subjects on the basis of being abnormal/degenerate and normal, those who are immune and those who are not, the multiplication of norms of life would break down such that all life would be respected in its singularity as life itself.

Law would no longer be an adversarial space that reconstructs positions of authority based on divisions between subjects; instead it would become a collective space of justice led by critical discussion rather than by formative persons. As with the judge who makes decisions and remains in the first and or second person (as a so-called interlocutor), appellants also remain in the first person through assisted dying appeals that are currently practices of rights. An appeal to a "right to die" in the language of rights has a "private and privative character" (Esposito, 2013: 119); it closes us off from one another before we have even entered into a realm of discussion (Weil, 1986). Law as critique and as a third person politics would not speak in or respond to the language of rights. Instead, law would serve as a critical space where justices and other parties would listen carefully to appellants, family members, as well as those who support or object to various practices. In doing so law would instead become a space for "critical dialogue" rather than "appeals" and "rights."

This critical dialogue that would replace "rights" appeals would view law as an important common space in which a review panel could be composed that is comprised of the subject themselves, the family members, alongside ethicists, lawyers, doctors and those intervenors who want to converse from different vantages. Such a review panel would have legal authority but with democratic, communal participation. This would be an ethical approach that recognizes the place of law and safeguards and the fact that one cannot "do away" with immunity per se, but that also recognizes the need for a more communal and open form of law: it would provide a safe space for a criticality and "thinking otherwise" regarding death that opens up to the challenges of a given time and place. It would also consider the voices of persons who are involved with the case and better consider the subject's request for assisted death as part of a community, the members of which will be impacted by such death. Gloria Taylor had noted, for instance, that she did not want to suffer in her death unnecessarily by being forced to live in pain without the possibility of reprieve toward the end of her life where she would not be in a state to end her life herself. Speaking to this anticipated pain and suffering she stated, " I do not want my life to end violently. I do not want my mode of death to be traumatic for my family members. I want the legal right to die peacefully, at the time of my own choosing, in the embrace of my family and friends" (*Carter v Canada*, 2015, paragraph 12). Taylor's case also discussed previous witnesses voiced in the affidavits of subjects who had described the alternative of assisted death as a premature suicide. As these witnesses stated, not only would this mean that subjects seeking assisted death might feel compelled to end their lives before they feel ready (hence before their body degenerates further), but it also enacts what many consider to be a cruelty to their families. As one witness noted: "I was going to blow my head off. I have a gun and I seriously considered doing it. I decided that I could not do that to my family. It would be horrible to put them through something like that ... I want a better choice than that" (*Carter v Canada*, 2015, paragraph 15).

Carter v Canada (2012, 2013, 2015), like many other cases, drew on affidavits to construct a decision on assisted dying, which therefore engages those outside of the immediate case in the broader discussion. However, engaging family members and other parties within a panel discussion itself that reviews the particulars of the case in concert could add to such a democratic, communal participation. Family members in the case of *Re E (Medical Treatment: Anorexia)* (2012), for example, had allegedly accepted E's immanent death and had supported her decision to enter palliative care. If family members had been involved in a review panel regarding the case, the Judge may have arrived at a very different conclusion than enforcing what some may regard as a paternalistic decision when he determined that E ought to be force-fed. Likewise, there may be instances in which appellants seek assisted death and a panel concludes that such a death may not in the first instance be most appropriate: perhaps, for example, one is presented with an elderly, terminally ill subject seeking assisted death and it is revealed that the subject has been suffering from long bouts of loneliness and social isolation. Assisted death is sought because everyday life feels unmanageable, lonely and the subject is lacking in social support. In this instance perhaps there are no family members on the review board but there is an attendant care worker in the home that the subject inhabits. If this case were presented for review, a panel that includes the care worker or other members of the care community might suggest instead that such a decision on assisted death is refused or postponed in the first instance until measures have been taken to address significant factors affecting the subject's life, such as facilitating and improving care facilities and social interactions through local service providers. This review panel would take a more particular approach to cases that treats each case as unique, and treats each of the subjects and the community surrounding the subject involved in the case as unique, drawing on precedent only in order to review and "extend" it (i.e. create new precedent). This approach would not impose a blanket ban on assisted death but, rather, by looking at the particulars of cases including the family and the social context in which the appellant is situated (including the care home for example in the case of elderly persons in social care), it would allow the law to become more responsive.

A more responsive law would become a more responsible law: this approach would not require a radical change or rewriting of statute on assisted dying (which would be a transcendental approach to imposing and applying new law paternalistically), but rather it would involve an immanent process of change through the creation of new norms from within the very system that currently circumscribes said norms. A more responsive law would require precisely what Esposito calls the multiplication of norms of life: rather than confining life within the limits of law's transcendental norm, it would open up this norm to the unpredictability of legal decisions that proliferate these norms from the inside-out.

Replacing Judges with Justices

If case law is also a third person it can no longer be regarded as judge-made law but rather is law as critique and the "judge" is simply justice. Judges are first persons; one cannot be an interlocutor and be a third person. Persons of justice are third persons (Esposito, 2012a: 115). The justices—and the panelists—would act as critics and would hold account of all arguments and deconstruct these arguments. The justices would not present a judgment through the simple application of precedent, as noted above, but instead would create new precedents in a space of justice that responds to the particularities of cases that would embrace critical openings for law. Justices would be comprised of those legal professionals who are trained in dialogue, not relying on statute or on precedent; they would be counselors of people who can arbitrate and help resolve conflict, listening to all parties and attempting to resolve a compromise based on the singularities presented before them.

Multiplying Social Norms and Subject Positions

With case law as critique, the judges as figures of justice, and appellants as those who open up critical dialogues, case law would deal with appeals to assisted death very differently. I have already noted how, when case law is opened up to deal with the particularities of cases, it means that those who engage in the dialogue of the case is opened up and also that the role of precedent can shift. A third person politics that tries to avoid the language of the personal would proliferate norms that make this attention to particularities a central issue. This could be done in several ways in assisted dying cases that responds to the main problems that the various chapters of this book have identified. For example, where chapters have noted that case law as it currently exists will endeavor to fix subject positions such that it can apply universal principles to these subjects, as a practice of critique and a third person politics, case law would find ways to ensure that subject positions are not fixed. Indeed, in opening up precedent and being critical of social norms that are entrenched in this precedent and in broader social issues brought to attention in the practice of law as critique, justices would aim to deal with the particularities of the case at hand.

Take, for example, the English case of Dianne Pretty. The judge was bound by *stare decisis* to apply *Bland*. Precedent argued that subjects could be "let die" but that "making die" was not a legal practice. Chapter 3 showed how the law then used the concept of inviolability of persons as a universalizing and particularizing tool to frame Pretty as a bordered subject whose body could not be violated by outside intrusion. The law fed the two legal fictions of the immune person and immune society that constituted Pretty in a relation of reciprocal dissociation, closed off from all other subjects through law's alleged benevolent paternalism. Her request for her husband to help her die was denied. Law as a third person politics would not blindly apply *Bland*. Not only would it recognize that the legal fictions created in Pretty's case that denied her the prospect of assistance in death did not treat her case on its own terms but also it would recognize that it did not deconstruct the ways that inviolability constrained and fed this pastoral logic of closure. One technique would be to ensure that subjects of assisted death are not fixed in particular ways. Deconstructing the link between Bland and Pretty, the law would show, as Chapter 3 did, how these differences between acts and omissions are sustained through fictions that are required for the universalizing possibility of law. If justice deals in particulars and not persons, justice cannot continue to fabricate fictions to sustain a truth that upholds divisive social norms.

In relation to Nicklinson's case discussed in Chapter 2 on enmity and vulnerability, law would have to consider how it has already fixed others as necessary enemies of appellants before they have had a chance to act. The law as a third person politics has a responsibility to deconstruct the ways that concepts of enmity and vulnerability are invoked in law to feed a fiction of persons who require protecting and immunizing from one another. A critical law would consider other possibilities that in paying attention to the individual case would deconstruct this logic. One could argue that many of the loved ones who would help subjects die are not inevitably trying to "get rid" of their family member who the law articulates as a burden and therefore as a necessary enemy (as with Fleming's case, discussed in Chapters 2 and 5); instead they could consider helping their loved ones die to be an act of love. In many instances, helping a loved one die is not a "relief" of burden on the subject who is left behind; it is not an act that restores one to oneself as a whole appropriated being, but it is a painful process. It might be better regarded as an expropriative act that takes one outside of one's self. Through the death of the other one does not become complete, returned to a whole that is immunized through the death of this other who was a burden; rather, one loses a part of oneself when one's loved one dies. Through the other's death one's self is expropriated (Noys, 2000). One could argue that "compassionate killing" is possible not as a measure of restoring one's self, but as a measure of opening this self up to the other.[2] In this regard there should be no reason why compassion is not viewed as a reasonable motive for ending life.

The case of *Rodriguez* discussed in Chapter 5 on dependency provides another example. Rodriguez vehemently claimed that she did not want to be a dependent subject and felt that the law that denied her assisted death depersonalized her. Requests to death on the basis of a relation between a subject position of dependency and the social norm that links dependency to degeneracy would be brought into discussion in a critical third person practice of law. The discussion, with the judge as justice, would consider how a request for an independent death is potentially a privatizing, personalizing appeal that feeds legal fictions of subjects who are reciprocally dissociated from one another. The justice would then engage in dialogue with the review panel around whether the request for death could be framed differently such that it could detach degeneracy from an inevitable link with dependency. Justices and other panelists might also consider how appeals to death could reinforce closures between requestors and others who would assist them based on social norms; however, it would also be considered how assisted death may not reinforce these closures but could instead become the very promise of an openness to otherness. For instance, panelists might instead engage in dialogue as to whether the practice of assisted death could be understood as a more originary kind of dependency relation: the requestor who appeals to assisted death is the requestor who is placing himself or herself in an absolutely dependent relation in seeking death with the help of another. Where at present the appeal for assisted death relied on a personalization via an appeal to "death with dignity" that appealed to a sovereign, independent death, we might instead consider how the notion of assistance in death reinforces the relationality of the act of assistance itself that also serves to deconstruct this sovereignty. Rather than a death with dignity being one that simply feeds a fiction of an immune person, a death with dignity via a request for assistance in death may reinforce the relationality of subjects. In this regard, a critical third person law would not simply close off assisted death as a practice; instead it would ask how assisted death is also currently confined to a norm of division between persons, as Chapter 2 on enmity and vulnerability, Chapter 3 on inviolability, Chapter 4 on security and as Chapter 5 on dependency showed.

Law as a practice of critique and a third person realm of justice is to deconstruct the legal fictions that sustain these divisions, and to open law out to the prospect of other ways of considering assisted death. These other prospects cannot be limited by concepts that feed fictions invoking closures. Rather, we could consider how these concepts also invoke an openness to community. For instance, Chapter 2 argued that law invoked the concept of vulnerability to frame particular kinds of subjects (requestors) as vulnerable to all others and to feed a legal fiction that rationalized the protection of these so called vulnerable persons. Chapter 2 also argued that a denial of this vulnerability is not a solution; an affirmative politics would not simply deny vulnerability within a critical legal realm. Nicklinson's denial of vulnerability, for instance, was problematic because it invoked the same legal fiction of an immune person, albeit from a different vantage: it continued to be a privatizing, personalizing politics. Instead one might consider how, rather than limiting vulnerability, one could proliferate it as a concept. Vulnerability cannot be attached to particular kinds of subjects; for example, as Chapter 5 demonstrated, we should avoid associating dependency with vulnerability. It reflects a wider neoliberal ethos that requires we be divided from one another as private subjects and therefore allows law to fix dependency and vulnerability as degenerate and abject because it apparently does not comport with this wider ethos. Working against the personalizing politics of a neoliberal ethos one might come to a more interconnected view of human lives that allows us to reframe vulnerability not as that which ought to distance us from one another (i.e., inevitably feed a legal fiction that closes us from one another) but rather considering how it might bring us together. The critical third person law would deconstruct the way concepts like vulnerability and dependency are used to shore up the limits of human relationships through the feeding of legal fictions that produce immune persons who are divided from one another. For instance, vulnerability might also be used to feed a fiction of a more open and relational politics. We might consider how each of us is vulnerable to one another and dependent on one another in a necessary way as part of our connectedness to one another (Butler, 2004; Olssen, 2010). Being vulnerable and dependent is not something we should remove ourselves from, but instead it is something that we all share in common as part of a web of connectedness (Butler, 2004; Olssen, 2010). Indeed this is the type of affirmative thinking that emerged in McLachlin's judgment in *Carter v Canada* (2015) at paragraph 87, noted in Chapter 4, in which we will recall that she emphasized the difficulty in "conclusively" identifying the vulnerable given the degree to which all persons are vulnerable. The role of law as a third person politics is to open up these possibilities; it is not simply to close off decisions by way of concepts that feed legal fictions reflecting social norms but instead it must consider how concepts could deconstruct these legal fictions and multiply social norms.

In multiplying social norms a critical third person space of law would refrain from fixing any possibility for assisted death within a particular subject position. It would not rationalize assisted death based on a personalizing politics at all but would find ways to open up politics to new rationales that were based on openings. One example might be that the law would treat requests to death from those who do not seem to be "degenerate enough" in a different way. For example Chapter 5 showed how the English law fixed E as the wrong kind of subject for death. The law cannot simply deny assisted death, nor can it legitimate it, on the basis of one's person: rather, the law would have to create or invent a different kind of politics to consider this prospect. Allowing the assisted death of subjects who do not appear to properly conform to the closed subjectivities of appellants the law currently regards as the right kind of subjects (e.g., dependents with no hope for a normal neoliberal life, as Chapter 5 discussed) might deconstruct the intimate link between being an abject subject and the desiring of death. In short, an affirmative politics of assisted death could not be contingent upon the subject position's "fixed identity" such that they fall into the category of being terminally ill, disabled or elderly but rather would be wholly based on the particularities of the case at hand.

Opening Up Who Can Assist with Death

In the same vein, the law must be open to the prospect that those who would assist in death cannot be fixed subjects either, and the law must respond to the prospect that not all persons who would take life are fixed. Taking cases as particularities, a critical third person space of law would try to expand and multiply the norm of who can be trusted. In being more open to these requests to death the law would also be required to be more open to the idea that people will help subjects die for benevolent reasons. Law ought not close off who can assist with death based on being certain kinds of subjects (e.g., medical practitioners versus a family member). Rather, the law might be more particular and moderate requests on a case-by-case basis, considering not "who" the assister is in terms of their credentials but "what" the assister reveals in terms of their motivations to help (Arendt, 1958). This also requires that norms of assistance are not enforced such that particular persons are left with the duty to take life but that all persons can potentially assist with death if considered singularly within the critical realm of law.

This does not mean that law should never deny a request to death. A critical law will make a decision based on the particulars of each case. However, this decision, always as a closure, would also always be reopened through a third person law as a practice of critique. My point is rather broader: law as a third person would open up legal cases as spaces of dialogue that not only proliferate norms via more diverse precedents based on the singularity of each legal case, but also would proliferate the subjectivities of those seeking assisted death and those who would offer to provide assisted death within its critical discussions; this would ensure that a critical law did not allow subjects to be fixed in categories such as vulnerable, enemies, degenerate, inviolable or secure persons.

Third Thesis: An Affirmative Law is an Open, Risky Law

One might argue that this is a risky kind of affirmative politics of assisted death but this is precisely the point. The role of law as critique would be to challenge the idea that law must invoke a problematic paternalism that serves as an inevitable closure; we do not need a law that grounds itself in such a negative view of humanity that allows it to rationalize its fictions of immune persons and an immune society that is required to protect us from one another. This closes off the potentials for how we can understand or interpret different ways that we act toward one another. For instance, Chapter 2 showed how the law rationalized certain acts of killing because they comported with the logic of protection and closure (e.g., self-defense and provocation) but did not recognize other acts that might be defined as compassionate.

A critical law of the third person cannot make subjects "known" in advance: we are not inherently defensive and privative; yet, law's paternal stance and the neoliberal ethos it brings into effect, currently tell us otherwise. How can we possibly trust one other and live reciprocally and relationally if we are already always divided from one another through laws that fix us in universalizing ways, claiming to know our intentions before we even act? While risky, a critical politics that deconstructs this link between knowable subjects and law is one way that the law might be able to open up new prospects. This is not to suggest that safeguards and law itself are not necessary; rather, it is to suggest that the law itself becomes more compassionate. Arguably, law that risks life is a more compassionate law. It is a law that is open to other prospects and open to community in a way that immunizing tenets of law through legal fictions that claim to allow the law to act in problematically paternal ways are not. Jean-Luc Nancy, for instance, suggests that compassion is "the contagion, the contact of being-with one-another in…turmoil. Compassion is not altruism, nor is it identification; it is the disturbance of violent relatedness" (Nancy, 2000: xiii). In the case of laws dealing with critical requests for assisted death one could imagine compassion as the exposure to the violent relatedness in the *munus*—not that with which we identify and therefore selectively choose—but as *compearance* or being-with that asks us to open ourselves up to the other (Nancy, 1993). Perhaps, then, a politics of assisted dying is precisely that which takes us outside of ourselves, providing the very openings for a new ethics and politics of relationality.

In short, critical case law is to become less normative in this process and instead become the proliferator of, and proliferation of, norms. In turn, this allows case law to become a new realm of justice that is immanent. It slowly brings the norms of the outside (i.e. neoliberal political rationality) in and challenges this outside, changing it over time by proliferating norms, breaking down the fictions of immune persons and immune society that sustain a reciprocally dissociative society. A society that instead proliferates norms of life disrupts mechanisms of immunization and opens out to new prospects of community. It grants more possibility for people to detach themselves from norms on the basis that they can live in particular ways. As Esposito recognizes, the "maximum deconstruction" of the immunitary paradigm rests precisely on the prospect of creating "continually new norms" (2008: 190).

To do so this involves an engagement of subjects with the law, as Hanafin, Patton and others point out, to allow the creation of new subjectivities. Through the process of subjectivation, subjects are able to relate to themselves in new ways by recognizing their relations to others, also in new ways. Law's fictions that currently create immune forms of person and politics can be opened up. One does not "replace" law's fictions with further fictions but rather one recognizes the roots of *all* law as fictive; such an approach then aims to play with the fictive nature of the law. This is not to suggest that we must create new legal fictions that do a better job of catering to particularities and interests of individuals; rather it is to suggest that we ought to allow the particularities of cases to break open the normativity of fictions that are currently sustained as truths and instead to reveal them for the fictions that they are. This of course burdens the law with more frequent need for review and attention to case particularities, but such a burden or dependency is precisely what this book is arguing in favor of. The law wants to detach itself from dependency of persons by universalizing itself as a totality, rationalizing this on account that it must apply equally to all, and detaching itself from the burden of attending to each; but this inevitably makes the law unable to effectively respond to the particularities of each case as it should.

In turn, the hope would be that a critical law of the third person, as a space of dialogue that is always open, would start to have an influence on the social conditions that exist outside of it. If law can act as a space that can deconstruct norms of society it can slowly work to reorient how we think about our relations to one another and the centrality of our dependency, rather than trying to remove ourselves from it. The outcome of this is unknowable: one might surmise that requests to assisted death might very well decline over time, or by way of contrast one might indeed find that requests proliferate. Esposito (2011: 27) writes:

> It would appear that to ensure common life, law is forced to put something inside it that maintains it beyond itself: to make it less common or not common- in other words, immune. But by immunizing life from community, law ends up sacrificing the intensity of life to the need for its preservation.

Moreover, as Georges Bataille has emphasized: "Communication cannot proceed from one full and intact individual to another. It requires individuals whose separate existence in themselves is risked, placed at the limit of death and nothingness" (Bataille, cited in Esposito, 2010: 145–146). To bring this book to a close—without immunizing, that is, closing off, the conclusion itself—one might ask the following open question: based on the conclusions that have emerged throughout, to what extent could the prospect of assisted dying be regarded not as a necessary closure, framed through immunizing concepts and legal fictions as the appeals and the legal denial of these appeals seem to be currently wedded, but rather as an openness to otherness that being-with and dying-with invokes as *possibility*?

Notes

1 This quote was accessed online: see Esposito, R. (2013). Community and nihilism, *Cosmos and History: The Journal of Natural and Social Philosophy* 5(1): http://cosmosandhistory.org/index.php/journal/article/view/124/234. See also Esposito, R. (2010). 'Appendix: Nihilism and community' in *Communitas*:

139. Here he offers a different variation on the quote: "Community is the 'with', the 'between', and the threshold where they meet in a point of contact that brings them into relation with others to the degree to which it separates them from themselves ... the being of community is the interval of difference, the spacing that brings us into relation with others in a common non-belonging, in this loss of what is proper that never adds up to a common 'good'."

2 In terms of the prospect of what right to die advocates often call "compassionate killing," this would involve a rethinking of compassion not as that which reifies divisions between subjects based on a "pity" for the other that depersonalizes this other and asserts our own proper status over this other, as Hannah Arendt's (2000 [1963]) reading of compassion would entail. From Arendt's vantage, for example, compassion is that which is 'stricken with the suffering of someone else as though it were contagious" (Arendt, 2000 [1963]: 75). Compassion keeps that other at a distance and is a vice of politics because it undermines solidarity and the prospect of political action. It does so because it is private and guided by our sentiments (Arendt, 2000 [1963]; Berlant, 2004; Kateb, 1984). Indeed this is akin to Judith Butler's (2004) point noted in Chapter 2, which is to suggest that compassion like the western liberal notion of vulnerability (that she wants to expand) is "selective" whereby we only help those who are in "proximity" to us. An affirmative politics of assisted dying grounded in compassion could not only respond to those of our choosing, in private, which would in turn allow us to remain closed off: this notion of compassion encourages us to remain in the first and second personal politics. Indeed one could note the very way that "conservative compassion" under the guise of liberal discourse often uses discourses of compassion to exert its own domination over other subjects (Butler and Athanasiou, 2013; Newcomb, 2007). One could interpret compassion as a dominant discourse that merely coincides with the neoliberal belief that persons are acting from a good moral vantage in killing their "loved" ones, when perhaps this disguises the way that we noted in previous chapters how individuals are part of a broader operation of power and internalization of this power: people believe they are being compassionate and acting benevolently, but at the same time are also articulating an inherent violence by reinforcing proper relational statuses (killing out of compassion in such a way that acts as a closure between subjects rather than as an opening). For instance, a subject might kill their loved one on the basis that the loved one wants to die independently and without burden; this might be interpreted then as a compassionate killing that reifies the immune community proper by reasserting divisions between subjects where neither subject is exposing themselves to an outside but is instead hypostatizing the already forged immune divisions. An affirmative politics of assisted dying would, like Nancy asserts, see compassion as something that exposes us to risk rather than that which feeds legal fictions of immune persons and an immune society.

References

Ackerman, F. (2000). For now I have my death: The 'duty to die' versus the duty to help the ill stay alive. *Midwest Studies in Philosophy* 24, 172–185.

Agamben, G. (1998). *Homo Sacer: Sovereign power and bare life*, Daniel Heller-Roazen (trans.), Stanford: Stanford University Press.

Amable, B. (2011). Morals and politics in the ideology of neo-liberalism. *Socio-Economic Review* 9(1), 3–30.

Amendola, A. (2012). The law of the living: Material for hypothesizing the biojuridical. *Law, Culture and the Humanities* 8(1), 102–118.

Amundson, R. and Taira, G. (2005). Our lives and ideologies. *Journal of Disability Policy Studies* 16(1), 53–57.

Arendt, H. (1958). *The Human Condition*, Chicago: University of Chicago Press.

Arendt, H. (2006 [1963]). *On Revolution*. London: Penguin Books.

Arrow, K.J. (1963). Uncertainty and the welfare economics of medical care. *The American Economic Review* 53, 941–973.

Barkan, J. (2012). Roberto Esposito's political biology and corporate forms of life. *Law, Culture and the Humanities* 8(1), 84–101.

Barnes, C. (1992). *Disabling Imagery and the Media: An exploration of the principles for media representations of disabled people*. Halifax, UK: Ryburn Publishing.

Barry, A., Osborne, T. and Rose, N. (eds) (1996). *Foucault and Political Reason: Liberalism, neo-liberalism and rationalities of government*, Chicago: Chicago University Press.

Bauman, Z. (2000). *Liquid Modernity*. Cambridge: Polity Press.

Baxter, K.I. (2012). Judging judgment in Chinua Achebe's *No Longer at Ease*. In M. Wan (ed.) *Reading the Legal Case: Cross currents between law and the Humanities*, New York: Routledge, 159–172.

Bayatrizi, Z. (2008). *Life Sentences: The modern ordering of mortality*. Toronto: University of Toronto Press.

Beeson, M. and Firth, A. (1998). Neoliberalism as a political rationality: Australian public policy since the 1980s. *Journal of Sociology* 34, 215–231.

Behuniak, S. (2011). Death with dignity: The wedge that divides the disability rights movement from the right to die movement. *Politics & The Life Sciences* 30(1), 17–32.

Berlant, L. (2004). *Compassion: The culture and politics of an emotion*. London: Routledge.

Biggs, S. and Powell, J. (2000). Surveillance and elder abuse: The rationalities and technologies of community care. *Journal of Contemporary Health* 4(1), 43–49.

Biggs, S. and Powell, J. (2001). A Foucauldian analysis of old age and the power of social welfare. *Journal of Aging & Social Policy* 12(2), 93–112.

Billings, A. and Block, S. (1996). Slow euthanasia, *Journal of Palliative Care* 12(4), 21–30.

Birnbacher, D. (2007). Terminal sedation, euthanasia, and causal roles. *Medscape General Medicine* 9(2), 48.

Bishop, J.P. (2006). Euthanasia, efficiency, and the historical distinction between killing a patient and allowing a patient to die. *Journal of Medical Ethics* 32(4), 220–224.

Bourdieu, P. (1992). The left hand and the right hand of the state. In G. Sapiro (ed.) *Acts of Resistance: Against the tyranny of the market*, New York: The New Press, 86–93.

Brandon, C. (1999). *The Electric Chair: An unnatural American history*. North Carolina: McFarland & Company.

Brewer, S. (1998). *The Philosophy of Legal Reasoning*. New York: Garland.

Brown, L. (2010). Stigma: an enigma demystified. In L.J. Davies (ed.) *The Disability Studies Reader*, London: Routledge Press, 147–160.

Brown, W. (1995). *States of Injury: Power and freedom in late modernity*. Princeton: Princeton University Press.

Brown, W. (2003). Neo-liberalism and the end of liberal democracy. *Theory & Event* 7(1), 1–19.

Brown, W. (2005). *Edgework: Critical essays on knowledge and politics*. Princeton: Princeton University Press.

Brunon-Ernst, A. (2013). *Beyond Foucault: New perspectives on Bentham's panopticon*. Surrey: Ashgate Publishing Limited.

Butler, J. (2004). *Precarious Life: The powers of mourning and violence*. London: Verso.

Butler, J. (2012). Adorno prize lecture: Can one lead a good life in a bad life? *Radical Philosophy*: www.egs.edu/faculty/judith-butler/articles/can-one-lead-a-good-life-in-a-bad-life/

Butler, J. and Athanasiou, A. (2013). *Dispossession: The performative in the political*, Cambridge, MA: Polity Press.

Callahan, D. (2008). Health care costs and medical technology. In M. Crowley (ed.) *From Birth to Death and Bench to Clinic: The Hastings Center bioethics briefing book for journalists, policymakers, and campaigns*, Garrison, NY: The Hastings Center, 79–82.

Campbell, F. (2005). Legislating disability: Negative ontologies and the government of legal identities. In S. Tremain (ed.) *Foucault and the Government of Disability*, Ann Arbor: University of Michigan Press, 170–204.

Campbell, T. (2008). Introduction. In R. Esposito (ed.) *Bios: Biopolitics and Philosophy*, Minneapolis: University of Minnesota Press, 3–12.

Campbell, T. (2010). "Foucault was not a person": Idolatry and the impersonal in Roberto Esposito's Third Person, *The New Centennial Review* 10(2), 135–150.

Campbell, T. (2011). *Improper life: Technology and life from Heidegger to Agamben*, Minnesota: University of Minnesota Press.

Campbell, T. (2012). Enough of a self: Esposito's impersonal biopolitics. *Law, Culture and the Humanities* 8(1), 31–46.

Campbell, T. (2013). Roundtable: Improper life: Technology and life from Heidegger to Agamben, *Law, Culture and the Humanities Conference*, Birkbeck Law School, London.

Campbell, T. and Luisetti, F. (2010). On contemporary French and Italian political philosophy: An interview with Roberto Esposito. *Minnesota Review* 109–118.

Campbell, T. and Sitze, A. (2013). *Biopolitics: A reader.* New York: Duke University Press Books.

Cassidy, J. (2010). Care not killing, *British Medical Journal,* 342 (7787), 29.

Cherny, N.I. and Radbruch, L. (2009). Board of the European Association for Palliative Care European Association for Palliative Care (EAPC) recommended framework for the use of sedation in palliative care. *Palliative Medicine* 23, 581–593.

Cholbi, M. (2010). The duty to die and the burdonsomeness of living. *Bioethics* 24: 412–420.

Colby, W. H. (2006) *Unplugged: Reclaiming our right to die in America.* New York: Amacom.

Corlett, J. A. (2001). Is there a moral duty to die? *Health Care Analysis* 9(1): 41–63.

Crouch, C. (2013). *The strange non-death of neoliberalism.* Cambridge: Polity Press.

Cruikshank, B. (1999). *The Will to Empower: Democratic citizens and other subjects.* Ithaca and London: Cornell University Press.

Davis, A. (2004). A disabled person's perspective on euthanasia. *Disability Studies Quarterly* 24(3) (online).

Dayan, C. (2011). *The Law is a White Dog: How legal rituals make and unmake persons.* Princeton: Princeton University Press.

Dean, M., Cellarius, V. and Oneshuk, D. (2012). Framework for continuous palliative sedation therapy in Canada, *Journal of Palliative Medicine* 15(8), 870–879.

Deigh, J. (1998). Physician assisted suicide and voluntary active euthanasia: some relevant differences. *The Journal of Criminal Law and Criminology* 88(3), 1155–1165.

Deleuze, G. and Guattari, F. (1991). *What is Philosophy?* New York: Columbia University Press.

Denike, M. (2000). Sexual violence and "fundamental justice": On the failure of equality reforms to criminal proceedings. *Canadian Woman Studies* 20(3), 151–159.

Derrida, J. (1991). *Given Time: 1. Counterfeit money.* Peggy Kamuf (Trans), Chicago and London: University of Chicago Press.

Derrida, J. (1995). *The Gift of Death.* Chicago: University of Chicago Press.

Derrida, J. (2000). *Of Hospitality.* Stanford: Stanford University Press.

Derrida, J. (2002). The animal that therefore I am (More to follow). *Critical Inquiry* 28(2), 369–418.

Derrida, J. (2004). *Rogues: Two essays on reason.* Stanford: Stanford University Press.

Derrida, J. (2009). *The Beast and the Sovereign Volume One,* Chicago and London: University of Chicago Press.

Dobinson, I. and Johns, F. (2007). Qualitative legal research. In Mike McConville and Wing Hong Chui (eds) *Research Methods for Law,* Edinburgh: Edinburgh University Press, 16–45.

Donzelot, J. and Gordon, C. (2008). Governing liberal societies: The Foucault effect in the English-speaking world. *Foucault Studies* 5, 48–62.

Douglas, C., Kerridge, I. and Ankeny, R. (2008). Managing intentions: The end of life administration of analgesics and sedatives, and the possibility of slow euthanasia. *Bioethics* 22, 388–396.

Dowbiggin, I. (2005). *A Concise History of Euthanasia: Life, death, God, and medicine.* Lanham, MD: Rowman & Littlefield.

Doyal, L. (2001). Editorial: Why active euthanasia and physician assisted suicide should be legalised, *British Medical Journal* 323: 1079.

Durkheim, E. (1979 [1897]). *Suicide: A Study in Sociology.* New York: The Free Press.

Dworkin, R. (1993). *Life's Dominion: An argument about abortion, euthanasia, and individual freedom.* London: Vintage Books, Random House.

Dworkin, R., Nagel, T., Rawls, R., Scanlon, T. and Jarvis Thompson, J. (1997). Assisted suicide: The philosopher's brief. *New York Review of Books* 27, 41–47.

Esposito, R. (2008). *Bios: biopolitics and philosophy,* Timothy Campbell (Trans), Introduction by Timothy Campbell, Minneapolis: University of Minnesota Press.

Esposito, R. (2010). *Communitas: The origin and destiny of community,* Timothy Campbell (Trans), Stanford: Stanford University Press.

Esposito, R. (2011). *Immunitas: The protection and negation of life,* Zakiya Hanafi (Trans), Cambridge: Polity Press.

Esposito, R. (2012a). The dispositif of the person. *Law, Culture and the Humanities* 8(1), 17–30.

Esposito, R. (2012b). *Third Person: Politics of life and philosophy of the impersonal.* Cambridge: Polity Press.

Esposito, R. (2012c). *Terms of the Political: Community, immunity, biopolitics,* Introduction by Vanessa Lemm, Rhiannon Noel Welch (Trans), Bronx, NY: Fordham University Press.

Esposito, R. and Paparcoe, A. (2006). Interview, *Diacritics* 36(2), 49–56.

Esposito, R. and Parsley, C. (2009). Preface to categories of the impolitical. *Diacritics* 39(2), 99–115.

Esposito, R., Nancy, J. and Campbell, T. (2010). Dialogue on the philosophy to come. *Minnesota Review* 75, 71–88.

Ewald, F. (1986). A social concept of law. In G. Teubner (ed.) *Dilemmas of Law in the Welfare State,* Berlin: de Gruyter, 40.

Ewald, F. (1990). Norms, discipline and the law, *Representations* 30, 138–161.

Ewig, C. (2011). *Second-wave Neoliberalism: Gender, race, and health sector reform.* University Park, PA: Penn State University Press.

Fagundes, D. (2001). Note, what we talk about when we talk about persons: The language of a legal fiction. *Harvard Law Review* 114, 1746–1752.

Feinburg, J. (1980). *Rights, Justice and the Bounds of Liberty.* Princeton: Princeton University Press.

Feinburg, J. (1986). *Harm to Self: The moral limits of the criminal law (Vol. 3),* New York: Oxford University Press.

Fennell, L.A. (2004). Relative burdens: Family and the safety net. *William & Mary Law Review* 45(4), 1453–1523.

Fine, R. (2005). From Quinlan to Schiavo: Medical, ethical, and legal issues in severe brain injury, *Baylor University Medical Centre Proceedings* 18(4), 303–310.

Flyvbjerg, B. (2000). *Ideal Theory, Real Rationality: Habermas versus Foucault and Nietzsche.* http://flyvbjerg.plan.aau.dk/IdealTheory.pdf

Foucault, M. (1972). *The Archaeology of Knowledge.* London: Tavistock Publications Limited.

Foucault, M. (1973). *The Birth of the Clinic: An archaeology of medical perception,* A.M. Sheridan Smith (Trans), New York: Pantheon.

Foucault, M. (1980). *Power/knowledge: Selected interviews and other writings 1972–1977.* Brighton: Harvester Press.

Foucault, M. (1981). Omnes et singulatim. In S. McMurrin (ed.) *The Tanner Lectures on Human Values (Vol 2),* Cambridge: Cambridge University Press, 233–254.

Foucault, M. (1982). The subject and power, *Critical Inquiry* 8(4), 777–795.

Foucault, M. (1984). Nietzsche, genealogy, history. In P. Rabinow (ed.) The Foucault Reader, New York: Pantheon, 76–100.

Foucault, M. (1988). The political technology of individuals. In: Luther Martin, Huck Gutman and Patrick Hutton (eds) *Technologies of the Self.* Massachusetts: University of Massachusetts Press, 145–162.

Foucault, M. (1990a). The History of Sexuality, volume 1: An introduction. New York: Random House.

Foucault, M. (1990b). Social security. In L. Kritzman (ed.) *Politics, Philosophy, Culture: Interviews and Other Writings, 1977–1984,* London: Routledge, 158–177.

Foucault, M. (1991a). Governmentality. In: G. Burchell, C. Gordon and P. Miller (eds) *The Foucault Effect. Studies in governmentality,* Chicago: Chicago University Press, 87–104.

Foucault, M. (1991b). Politics and the study of discourse. In G. Burchell, C. Gordon and P. Miller (eds) *The Foucault Effect: Studies in governmentality,* Chicago: Chicago University Press, 53–72.

Foucault, M. (1991c). Questions of method. In G. Burchell, C. Gordon and P. Miller (eds) *The Foucault Effect: Studies in governmentality,*Chicago: Chicago University Press, 73–86.

Foucault, M. (1996a). The simplest of pleasures. In S. Lotringer (ed.) *Foucault Live (interviews, 1961–1984)*, New York: Semiotext(e), 295–297.

Foucault, M. (1996b). The social extension of the norm. In S. Lotringer (ed.) *Foucault Live (interviews, 1961–1984)*, New York: Semiotext(e), 196–199.

Foucault, M. (1997). What is critique? In S. Lotringer (ed.) *The Politics of Truth,* Los Angeles, CA: Semiotext(e), 41–81.

Foucault, M. (2003). Society Must be Defended: Lectures at the College de France, 1975–76. D. Macey (Trans), New York: Picador.

Foucault, M. (2007). Security, Territory, Population: Lectures at the College de France, 1977–78. G. Burchell (Trans), New York: Palgrave Macmillan.

Foucault, M. (2008). The Birth of Biopolitics: Lectures at the College de France, 1978–79. G. Burchell (Trans), New York: Palgrave Macmillan.

Frank, J.B. (1976). Body snatching: A grave medical problem. *Yale Journal of Biology and Medicine* 49(4), 399–410.

Friedland, R. and Robertson, A. (1990). *Beyond the Marketplace: Rethinking economy and society.* New York: Walter de Gruyter.

Friedlander, H. (1995). *The Origins of Nazi Genocide: From euthanasia to the final solution.* Chapel Hill: University of North Carolina Press.

Fuller, L. (1967). *Legal Fictions.* Stanford: Stanford University Press.

Gane, N. (2012). The governmentalities of neoliberalism: Panopticism, post-panopticism and beyond. *The Sociological Review* 60(4), 611–634.

Ganzini, L., Goy, E. and Dobscha, S. (2008). Prevalence of depression and anxiety in patients requesting physicians' aid in dying: Cross sectional survey. *British Medical Journal* 337, 1682.

Garrard, E. and Wilkinson, S. (2005). Clinical ethics: Passive euthanasia. *Journal of Medical Ethics* 31, 64–68.

Gauthier, S., Mausbach, J., Reisch, T. and Bartsch, C. (2014). Suicide tourism: A pilot study on the clinical phenomenon. *Journal of Medical Ethics*, Published Online First: doi:10.1136/medethics-2014-102091.

Gershon, I. and Alexy, A. (2011). Special collection: The ethics of disconnection in a neoliberal age (Introduction), *Anthropological Quarterly* 84 (4), 799–808.

Gillon, R. (1985). An introduction to philosophical medical ethics: The Arthur case. *British Medical Journal* 290, 1117.

Glasgow, S.M. (2012). The politics of self-craft: Expert patients and the public health management of chronic disease, *Sage Open* 1–11.

Glynos, J. (2013). Neoliberalism, markets, fantasy: The case of health and social care. *Psychoanalysis, Culture & Society*, 19(1), 5–12.

Goffman, E. (2010). *Relations in Public: Microstudies of the public order*. New Brunswick: Transaction Publishers.

Golder, B. (2011). Foucault's critical (yet ambivalent) affirmation: Three figures of rights, *Social & Legal Studies* 20(3), 283–312.

Golder, B. (2013). *Re-reading Foucault: On law, power and rights*. Abington: Routledge.

Golder, B. and Fitzpatrick, P. (2009). *Foucault's Law*. Abington: Routledge.

Goodrich, P. (2012). The theatre of emblems: On the optical apparatus and the investiture of persons. *Law, Culture and the Humanities* 8(1), 47–67.

Gordon, C. (1991). Governmental rationality: An introduction. In: G. Burchell, C. Gordon and P. Miller (eds) *The Foucault Effect. Studies in governmentality*, Chicago: Chicago University Press, 1–52.

Hamilton, J. (2013). *Security: Politics, humanity, and the philology of care*. Princeton: Princeton University Press.

Hamman, J. (2009). Neoliberalism, governmentality and ethics. *Foucault Studies* 6, 37–59.

Hanafin, P. (2003). Surviving law: Death, community, culture. In A. Sarat (ed.) *Studies in Law and Politics, Volume 28*. Bingley, UK: Emerald Group Publishing Limited, 97–115.

Hanafin, P. (2007). *Conceiving life: Reproductive politics and the law in contemporary Italy*, Hampshire, England: Ashgate Publishing.

Hanafin, P. (2009). Refusing disembodiment: Abortion and the paradox of reproductive rights in contemporary Italy, *Feminist Theory* 10(2), 227–244.

Hanafin, P. (2011). The embryonic sovereign meets the biological citizen: The biopolitics of reproductive rights: http://backdoorbroadcasting.net/2011/11/patrick-hanafin-the-embryonic-sovereign-meets-the-biological-citizen-the-biopolitics-of-reproductive-rights/

Hanafin, P. (2014). Resistant lives: Law, life, singularity, *Soft Power* 1(1), 91–107: www.softpowerjournal.com/web/wp-content/uploads/2014/10/articolo-6-Resistent-lives.pdf

Hardes, J. (2013). Fear, sovereignty and the right to die, *Societies* 3(1), 66–79.

Hardes, J. (2014). Biopolitics and the enemy: On law, rights and proper subjects, *Law, Culture and the Humanities Journal*. Forthcoming. Online before print, doi: 10.1177/1743872114524879.

Hardes, J., McLane, P. and Pavlich, G. (2014). Personhood, legal judgment, and sovereignty at the Cape, 1793–1810. *The Routledge Handbook of International Crime and Justice Studies*, London: Routledge, 612–632.

Hardwig, J. (1997). Is there a duty to die? *Hastings Centre Report* 27:34–42:34.

Hardwig, J. (2002). Dying at the right time: Reflections on assisted and unassisted suicide. In H. LaFollette, (ed.) *Ethics in Practice*, New York: Blackwell, 48–58.

Hart, H.L.A. (1982). *Essays on Bentham: Jurisprudence and political philosophy*. Oxford: Oxford University Press.

Harvey, D. (2005). *A Brief History of Neoliberalism*. Oxford: Oxford University Press.

Haughton, S. (1866). On hanging considered from a mechanical and physiological point of view. *London, Edinburgh and Dublin Philosophical Magazine and Journal of Science* 32(213).

Hayry, H. and Hayry, M. (1990). Euthanasia, ethics and economics. *Bioethics* 4(2), 154–161.

Heasell, S. and Paton, D. (2001). Economics and euthanasia, *Health Service Management Research* 14(1), 62–63.

Hepworth, M. (1996). William and the old folks: Notes on infantilisation. *Ageing and Society* 16(4), 423–452.

Heyer, K. (2011). Rejecting rights: The disability critique of physician assisted suicide. In Austin Sarat (ed.) *Special Issue Social Movements/Legal Possibilities, Studies in Law, Politics, and Society* 54, 77–112.

Hirschl, R. (2000). "Negative" rights vs. "positive" entitlements: A comparative study of judicial interpretations of rights in an emerging neo-liberal economic order, *Human Rights Quarterly* 22(4), 1060–1098.

Hiranandani, V. (2005). Towards a critical theory of disability in social work. *Critical Social Work* 6(1): www1.uwindsor.ca/criticalsocialwork/towards-a-critical-theory-of-disability-in-social-work

House of Lords (1994). *Report of the House of Lords Select Committee on Medical Ethics HL Paper 21-1*. London: House of Lords.

Humphry, D. (1991). *Final Exit: The practicalities of self-deliverance and assisted suicide for the dying*. New York: Dell Publishing, Random House.

Humphry, D. (2005). *The Good Euthanasia Guide: Where, what and who in choices in dying*. Norris Lane: Norris Lane Press.

Hunt, A. and Wickham, G. (1994). *Foucault and Law: Towards a sociology of law as governance*. London: Pluto Press.

Huxtable, R. (2002). D(en)ying life: The sanctity of life doctrine in English law, *Retfærd* 25(3), 60–81.

Joronen, M. (2013). Conceptualising new modes of state governmentality: Power, violence and the ontological mono-politics of neoliberalism. *Geopolitics* 18(2), 356–370.

Kantorowicz, E. (1997). *The Kings Two Bodies: A study in mediaeval political theology*. Princeton: Princeton University Press.

Karma, H. (2005). Female (?) knowledge, normativity and legal interpretation. *No Foundations: An Interdisciplinary Journal of Law and Justice* 1, 3–11.

Kateb, G. (1984). *Hannah Arendt: Politics, conscience, evil (philosophy and society)*, Lanham: Rowman & Littlefield.

Keating, H. and Bridgeman, J. (2012) Compassionate killings: The case for a partial defence. *The Modern Law Review* 75(5), 697–721.

Kenner, A.M. (2008). Securing the elderly body: Surveillance, and the politics of "ageing in place", *Surveillance & Society* 5(3), 252–269.

Kissel, J. (2000). Grandma, the GNP and the duty to die: Is there a duty to die? In: J. Humber and R. Almeder (eds) *Is there a Duty to Die?* New York: Humana Press, 191–203.

Knauer, N. (2010). Legal fictions and juristic truth, *St. Thomas Law Review* 23(1), 1–51.

Kutner, L. (1969). Due process of euthanasia: The living will, a proposal. *Indiana Law Journal* 44 (4), 539–544.

Lacey, N. (2001a). In search for the responsible subject: History, philosophy and criminal law theory, *Modern Law Review* 64, 350–371.

Lacey, N. (2001b). Responsibility and modernity in criminal law, *Journal of Political Philosophy* 9, 249–277.

Lacey, N. (2007). Character, capacity, outcome: Toward a framework for assessing the shifting pattern of criminal responsibility in modern English law. In M. Dubber and L. Farmer (eds) *Modern Histories of Crime and Punishment*, Stanford: Stanford University Press, 14–41.

Lacey, N. (2008). Philosophy, political morality and history: Explaining the enduring resonance of the Hart-Fuller debate, *New York University Law Review* 83, 1059.

Lacey, N. (2009). Historicising criminalisation: Conceptual and empirical issues, *Modern Law Review* 72, 936.

Lacey, N. (2013). The jurisprudential annual lecture 2013: Institutionalising responsibility: Implications for jurisprudence, *Jurisprudence* 4(1), 1–19.

Landman, W. (2001). A proposal for legalizing assisted suicide and euthanasia in South Africa. In L. Koppelman and K. de Ville (eds) *Physician Assisted Suicide: What are the issues?* Dordrecht: Klewer Academic Publishers, 203–226.

Lanza-Kaduse, L. and Bishop, D. (1986). Legal fictions and criminology: The jurisprudence of drunk driving, *Journal of Criminal Law and Criminology* 77(2), 358–378.

Larner, W. (2000). Neoliberalism: Policy, ideology, governmentality. *Studies in Political Economy* 63, 5–25.

Lasch, C. (1991). *The Culture of Narcissism: American life in an age of diminishing expectations*, London and New York: W.W. Norton & Company (revised edition).

Lavi, S. (2008). *The Modern Art of Dying: A history of euthanasia in the United States.* Princeton: Princeton University Press.

Lefebvre, A. (2005). A new image of law: Deleuze and jurisprudence. *Telos* 130, 103–126.

Lefebvre, A. (2008). *The Image of Law: Deleuze, Bergson, Spinoza.* Stanford: Stanford University Press.

Lemke, T. (1997). *The Birth of Biopolitics: Michel Foucault's lecture at the College de France on neo-liberal governmentality*: www.thomaslemkeweb.de/engl.%20texte/The%20Birth%20of%20Biopolitics%203.pdf

Lemke, T. (2000). *Foucault, Governmentality, and Critique*: www.andosciasociology.net/resources/Foucault$2C+Governmentality$2C+and+Critique+IV-2.pdf

Lemke, T. (2001). The birth of biopolitics: Michel Foucault's lecture at the College de France on neo-liberal governmentality. *Economy & Society* 3(2), 190–207.

Lemke, T. (2002). Foucault, governmentality and critique. *Rethinking Marxism* 14(3), 49–64.

Lemke, T. (2011). *Biopolitics: An advanced introduction.* New York: New York University Press.

Lemm, V. (2012). Introduction to Roberto Esposito, *Terms of the Political: Community, Immunity, Biopolitics*, Rhiannon Noel Welch (Trans), New York: Fordham University Press.

Lemmens, T. and Dickens, B. (2001). Canadian law on euthanasia: Contrasts and comparisons, *European Journal of Health Law* 8, 135–155.

Leier, B. (2013). *Assisted Suicide in Canada: Why physicians should not kill their patients.* Presentation at the John Dossetor Health Ethics Centre, May 2 2013, University of Alberta.

Lero, D., Pletch, C. and Hilbrecht, M. (2012). Introduction to the special issue on disability and work: Toward re-conceptualizing the "burden" of disability, *Disability Studies Quarterly*, 32 (online).

Lifton, R. (2000). *The Nazi Doctors: Medical killing and the psychology of genocide.* New York: Basic Books.

Lopez, M. (2013). Hegel on communitas: An unexplored relationship between Hegel and Esposito, *Angelaki: Journal of the Theoretical Humanities* 18(3), 13–31.

Lupton, J. (2012). Arendt in Italy: Or, the taming of the shrew. *Law, Culture and the Humanities* 8(1), 68–83.

MacPherson, C.B. (1962). *The Political Theory of Possessive Individualism: Hobbes to Locke*, Oxford: Oxford University Press.

Maine, H. (1861). *Ancient Law: Its connection with the early history of society and relation to modern ideas.* London: Murray.

Marshall, T. (1995). *Murdering to Dissect: Grave robbing, Frankenstein, and the anatomy literature.* Manchester: Manchester University Press.

Martin, B. (2010). Techniques to pass on: technology and euthanasia, *Bulletin of Science, Technology and Societ*, 30(1), 54–59.

Mathiesen, T. (1997). The viewer society: Michel Foucault's panopticon revisited. *Theoretical Criminology* 1(2), 215–234.

Mauss, M. (1990 [1925]). *The Gift: The form and reason for exchange in archaic societies*, W.D. Halls (Trans), New York: W.W. Norton Incorporated.

May, T. (2012). *Friendship in an Age of Economics: Resisting the forces of neoliberalism.* Lanham, MD: Lexington Books.

McClain, L. C. (1995). Inviolability and privacy: The castle, the sanctuary and the body. *Yale Journal of Law & The Humanities* 7(1), 195–242.

McGee, A. (2014). Does withdrawing life-sustaining treatment cause death or allow the patient to die? *Medical Law Review* 22(1), 26–47.

McRuer, R. (2006). *Crip Theory: cultural signs of queerness and disability.* New York: New York University Press.

McNay, L. (2009). Self as enterprise: Dilemmas of control and resistance in Foucault's *The Birth of Biopolitics, Theory, Culture & Society* 26(6), 55–77.

McWhorter, L. (2005). Foreword. In: S. Tremain, *Foucault and the Government of Disability.* Michigan: Michigan University Press, xiii–xvii.

Michalowski, S. (2012). Relying on common law defences to legalise assisted dying: Problems and possibilities, *Medical Law Review* 0, 1–34.

Mihic, S. (2008). Neoliberalism and the jurisprudence of privacy: An experiment in feminist theorizing, *Feminist Theory* 9(2), 165–184.

Miles, S. (2006). *Oath Betrayed: Torture, medical complicity, and the war on terror.* New York: Random House.

Miller, F. and Truog, R. (2011). *Death, Dying and Organ Transplantation: Reconstructing medical ethics at the end of life.* Oxford: Oxford University Press.

Miller, F., Truog, R. and Brock, D. (2010). Moral fictions and medical ethics, *Bioethics* 24(9), 453–460.

Mills, C. (2010). Continental philosophy and bioethics, *Editorial: Bioethical Inquiry* 7, 145–148.

Morrison, W. (ed.) (2013). *Blackstone's Commentaries on the Laws of England, Volume III.* London: Cavendish Publishing Ltd.

Murray, S. (2007). Care and the self: Biotechnology, reproduction and the good life, *Philosophy, Ethics, and Humanities in Medicine,* 2(6), www.peh-med.com/content/pdf/1747-5341-2-6.pdf).

Naffine, N. (2003). Who are law's persons? From Cheshire cats to responsible subjects, *The Modern Law Review* 66(3), 346–367.

Naffine, N. (2009). *Law's Meaning of Life: Philosophy, religion, Darwin and the legal person.* Oxford: Hart Publishing.

Nancy, J.L. (1993). The Compearance: From the existence of communism to the community of existence, *Political Theory* 20(3), 371–398.

Nancy, J.L. (2000). *Being Singular Plural.* Stanford: Stanford University Press.

Nedelsky, J. (1990). Law, boundaries and the bounded self, *Special Issue: Representations: Law and the Order of Culture* 30, 162–189.

Nedelsky, J. (2012). *Law's Relations: A relational theory of self, autonomy, and law.* Oxford: Oxford University Press.

Newcomb, M. (2007). Totalized compassion: The (im)possibilities for acting out of compassion in the rhetoric of Hannah Arendt, *JAC* 27(1–2), 105–123.

New York Task Force on Life and Law (1994). *When Death is Sought: Assisted suicide and euthanasia in the medical context.* New York: New York State Task Force on Life and the Law.

Noys, B. (2000). *The Culture of Death.* Oxford: Berg.

Noys, B. (2005). *The Culture of Death.* New York: Berg.

Nuland, S.B. (1993). *How We Die: Reflections on life's final chapter.* New York: Random House.

O'Byrne, A. (2013). Communitas and the problem of women, *Angelaki: Journal of Theoretical Humanities* 18(3), 125–138.

Ogden, R.D. (2001). Non-physician assisted suicide: The technological imperative of the deathing counterculture, *Death Studies* 25, 387–401.

Oliva, R.B. (2006). From the immune community to the communitarian immunity: On the recent reflections of Roberto Esposito, *Diacritics* 36(2), 70–82.

Oliver, M. (1990). *The Politics of Disablement.* London: MacMillan.

Olivier, P. (1975). *Legal Fictions in Practice and Legal Science.* Rotterdam: Rotterdam University Press.

Olssen, M. (2010). *Liberalism, Neoliberalism, Social Democracy: Thin communitarian perspectives on political philosophy and education.* London: Routledge.

Orentlicher, D. (1997). The supreme court and terminal sedation: Rejecting assisted suicide, embracing euthanasia, *Hastings Constitutional Law Quarterly* 24, 947–968.

Packer, H. (1968). *The Limits of the Criminal Sanction.* Stanford: Stanford University Press.

Parkinson, C. and Howarth, C. (2008). The language of social entrepreneurs, *Entrepreneurship and Regional Development*, 20: 285–309.

Passas, N. (2000). Global anomie, dysnomie and economic crime: Hidden consequences of neoliberalism and globalization in Russia and around the world, *Social Justice* 27(2), 16–44.

Patton, P. (2012). Immanence, transcendence and the creation of rights. In L. de Sutter and K. McGee (eds) *Deleuze and Law,* Edinburgh: Edinburgh University Press, 15–31.

Pavlich, G. (1992). Mediating community disputes: The regulatory logic of government through pastoral power, PhD Dissertation, University of British Columbia..

Pavlich, G. (1995). Contemplating a postmodern sociology: Genealogy, limits and critiques, *The Sociological Review* 43(3), 548–572.

Pavlich, G. (1996). *Justice Fragmented: Mediating community disputes under postmodern conditions.* London: Routledge.

Pavlich, G. (2001). The art of critique or how not to be governed thus. In: G. Wickham and G. Pavlich (eds) *Rethinking Law, Society and Governance: Foucault's bequest.* Oxford: Hart Publishing, 141–154.

Pavlich, G. (2002). Towards an ethics of restorative justice. In: L. Walgrave, (ed.) *Restorative Justice and the Law.* Portland: Willan Publishing, 1–18.

Pavlich, G. (2004). What are the dangers as well as the promises of community involvement? In: H. Zehr and B. Toews (eds) *Critical Issues in Restorative Justice.* Monsey, New York and Cullompton, Devon, UK: Criminal Justice Press and Willan Publishing, 173–184.

Pavlich, G. (2005). Experiencing critique, *Law & Critique* 16, 95–112.

Pavlich, G. (2007). Deconstruction. In G. Ritzer (ed.) *Blackwell Encyclopaedia of Sociology.* Oxford: Blackwell, 1–16.

Pavlich, G. (2012a). Cape legal idioms and the colonial sovereign, *International Journal of the Semiotics of Law,* 26(1), 39–54.

Pavlich, G. (2012b). Legal judgment and Cape colonial law, *Law, Culture and the Humanities* 8(2), 207–218.

Pavlich, G. (2013). Criminal justice and Cape law's persons, *Social & Legal Studies,* 23(1), 55–72.

Pelaprat, E. and Hartouni, V. (2012). The cerebral subject in popular culture and the "end of life". In: Wolfgang Sützl and Theo Hug (eds) *Activitist Media and Biopolitics: Critical media interventions in the age of biopower.* Innsbruck: Innsbruck University Press, 191–204.

Pellizzoni, L. (2012). In search of community: Political consumerism, governmentality, and immunization, *European Journal of Social Theory* 15(2), 221–241.

Peredo, A. (2011). Social entrepreneurship. In L. Dana (ed.) *International Encyclopaedia of Entrepreneurship,* Cheltenham: Edwar Elgar, 410–414.

Peters, M.A. (2001). *Poststructuralism, Marxism and neoliberalism: Between theory and politics.* New York: Rowman and Littlefield.

Pfaff, H., Driller, E., Ernstmann, N., Karbach, U., Kowalski, C., Schiebler, F. and Ommen, O. (2010). Standardization and individualization of care for the elderly: Proactive behaviour through individualized standardization, *Open Longevity Science* 4, 51–57.

Phillipson, C. (1998) *Reconstructing Old Age.* London: Sage.

Picciotto, S. (1999). Offshore: The state as legal fiction. In: J. Abbott and M.

Hampton (eds) *Offshore Finance Centres and Tax Havens: The rise of global capital.* Basingstoke: Macmillan, 43–78.

Plaxton, M. (2008). Foucault, Agamben, and Arbour J.'s dissent in Gosselin, *Canadian Journal of Law and Jurisprudence* 21(2), 411–428.

Pothier, D. and Devlin, R. (2006). *Critical disability: Essays in philosophy, politics, policy and law.* Vancouver: UBC Press.

Powell, J.L. (2001). Theorizing gerontology: The case of old age, professional power and social policy in the United Kingdom, *Journal of Aging & Identity* 6(3), 117–135.

Powell, J. L. and Biggs, S. (2003). Foucauldian gerontology: A methodology for understanding aging, *Electronic Journal of Sociology*, 7(2): http://sociology.org/content/vol7.2/03_powell_biggs.html

Putnam, R. (2000). *Bowling Alone: The collapse and revival of American community.* New York: Simon & Schuster.

Quill, T., Lo, B. and Brock, D. (1997). Palliative options of last resort. A comparison of voluntary stopping eating and drinking, terminal sedation, physician assisted suicide and voluntary active euthanasia, *The Journal of the American Medical Association* 278, 2099– 2100.

Quill T., Coombs, L. and Nunn, S. (2000). For the University of Pennsylvania Center for Bioethics Assisted Suicide Consensus Panel Palliative treatments of last resort: choosing the least harmful alternative, *Annals of Internal Medicine*, 132488–132493.

Read, J. (2009). A genealogy of homo economicus: Neoliberalism and the production of subjectivity, *Foucault Studies* 6, 25–36.

Richardson, R. (1987). *Death, Dissection and the Destitute.* London and New York: Routledge and Kegan Paul.

Rivett, A. (2005). Right to die. No man (or woman) is an island, *British Medical Journal* 11; 330(7504), 1388–1389.

Rose, N. (1993). Government, authority, and expertise in advanced liberalism, *Economy & Society* 22(3), 283–299.

Rose, N. (1996a). Governing advanced liberal democracies. In A. Barry, T. Osborne and N. Rose (eds) *Foucault and Political Reason: Liberalism, neoliberalism and rationalities of government.* London: UCL Press, 37–64.

Rose, N. (1996b). The death of the social? Re-figuring the territory of government, *Economy and Society* 25(3), 327–356.

Rose, N. (1999). *Powers of Freedom: Reframing political thought.* Cambridge: Cambridge University Press.

Rose, N. (2001). The politics of life itself, *Theory, Culture and Society* 18(6), 1–30.

Rose, N. (2007). *The Politics of Life Itself: Biopower, medicine, and subjectivity in the twenty-first century.* Princeton: Princeton University Press.

Rose, N. and Novas, C. (2008). Biological citizenship. In A. Ong and S.J. Collier (eds) *Global Assemblages: Technology, politics, and ethics as anthropological problems*, Oxford: Blackwell, 439–464.

Rose, N. and Valverde, M. (1998). Governed by law? *Social & Legal Studies* 7(4), 541–551.

Saad-Filho, A. and Johnston, D. (2005). *Neoliberalism: A critical reader.* London: Pluto Press.

Saltes, N. (2013). "Abnormal" bodies on the borders of inclusion: Biopolitics and the paradox of disability surveillance, *Surveillance & Society* 11(1/2), 55–73.

Samuels, A. (1996). The advance directive (or living will), *Medicine, Science and the Law* 36(1), 2–8.

Sarratt, J. (2012). Autistic human rights: A proposal, *Disability Studies Quarterly* 32(4), (online).

Schane, S. (1987). The corporation is a person: The language of a legal fiction, *Tulsa Law Review* 61, 563–565.

Sennett, R. (2003). *Respect in a World of Inequality*. London: Penguin.

Shah, S. and Miller, F. (2010). Can we handle the truth? Legal fictions in the determination of death, *American Journal of Law and Medicine* 36, 540–585.

Singer, P. (1994). *Rethinking Life and Death: The collapse of our traditional ethics*. New York: St Martin's Press.

Singer, P. (2005). *The Sanctity of Life*: www.foreignpolicy.com/articles/2005/08/30/the_sanctity_of_life

Smith, C. (2000). The sovereign state v Foucault: Law and disciplinary power, *The Sociological Review* 48(2), 283–306.

Smith, W. (2006). *Forced Exit: Euthanasia, assisted suicide and the new duty to die*. New York: Encounter Books.

Somerville, M. (2001). *Death Talk: The case against euthanasia and physician assisted suicide*. Quebec: McGill-Queen's Press.

Sonntag, J. (2008). Doctor's involvement in torture, *Torture* 18(3), 161–175.

Sprung, C.L., Eidelman, L.A. and Steinberg, A. (1997). Is the patient's right to die evolving into a duty to die?: Medical decision making and ethical evaluations in health care, *Journal of Evaluation in Clinical Practice* 3(1), 69–75.

Sprung, C.L., Ledoux, H. and Bulow, H. (2008). Relieving suffering or intentionally hastening death: Where do you draw the line? *Critical Care Medicine* 36, 8–13.

Stevenson, J., Harp, B. and Gernsbacher, M.A. (2011). Infantilizing autism, *Disability Studies Quarterly*, 31(3), (online).

Stygall, G. (1994). *Trial Language: Differential discourse processing and discursive formation*. Philadelphia, PA: John Benjamins Publishing.

Swiffen, A. (2011). *Law, Ethics and the Biopolitical*. London: Routledge.

Tadros, V. (1998). Between governance and discipline: The law and Michel Foucault, *Oxford Journal of Legal Studies* 18 (1), 75–103.

Tännsjö, T. (2004). *Terminal Sedation: Euthanasia in disguise?* Netherlands: Springer.

Taylor, S. (2011). Beasts of burden: Disability studies and animal rights, *QuiParle* 19(2), 191–222.

Tierney, T. (1999). The preservation and ownership of the body. In G. Weiss and H. Fern Haber (eds) *Perspectives on Embodiment: The intersections of nature and culture*. New York: Routledge, 233–261.

Tierney, T. (2006). Suicidal thoughts: Hobbes, Foucault and the right to die, *Philosophy & Social Criticism* 32(5), 601–638.

Tierney, T. (2010). The governmentality of suicide: Peuchet, Marx, Durkheim and Foucault, *Journal of Classical Sociology* 10(4), 357–389.

Tong, R. (2000). Duty to die. In J. Humber and R. Almeder (eds) *Is there a Duty to Die?* New York: Humana Press, 133–158.

Townsend, P. (1981). The structured dependency of the elderly: A creation of social policy in the 20th Century, *Ageing and Society* 1, 5–28.

Tremain, S. (2005). *Foucault and the Government of Disability*. Michigan: Michigan University Press.

Turner, D. and Stagg, K. (2006). *Social Histories of Disability and Deformity.* Oxon: Routledge Press.
Valverde, M. (2003). *Law's Dream of a Common Knowledge.* Princeton: Princeton University Press.
Valverde, M. (2010). Specters of Foucault in Law and Society scholarship, *Annual Review of Law and Social Science* 6, 45–59.
Valverde, M. (2011). Questions of security: A framework for research, *Theoretical Criminology* 15(1), 3–22.
Vaz, P. and Bruno, F. (2003). Types of self-surveillance: From abnormality to individuals at risk, *Surveillance and Society* 1(3), 272–291.
Wacquant, L. (2010). Crafting the neoliberal state: Workforce, prisonfare and social insecurity, *Sociological Forum* 25(2), 197–220.
Waldron, J. (2009). *Dignity, Rank, and Rights: The 2009 Tanner Lectures at UC Berkeley.* New York University Public Law and Legal Theory Working Papers, paper 151, http://lsr.nellco.org/cgi/viewcontent.cgi?article=1150&context=nyu_plltwp
Waldschmidt, A. (2006). Normalcy, bio-politics and disability: Some remarks on the German disability discourse, *Disability Studies Quarterly*, 26(2), (online).
Walker, A. (1982). Dependency and old age, *Social Policy and Administration* 16, 115–135.
Webley, L. (2010). Qualitative approaches to empirical legal research. In: P. Cane and H. Kritzer (eds) *The Oxford Handbook of Empirical Legal Research.* Oxford: Oxford University Press, 926–949.
Weil, S. (1986). *Simone Weil: An anthology.* S. Miles (ed.). London: Penguin
Wennberg, R.N. (1989). *Terminal Choices: Euthanasia, suicide, and the right to die.* Michigan: Erdmans Publishing.
Whiting, R. (2002). *A Natural Right to Die: Twenty-three centuries of debate.* Westport: Greenwood Press.
Whitman, J. (2003). On Nazi honor and the "new" European dignity. In: C. Joerges and N. Ghaleigh (eds) *Darker Legacies of Law in Europe: The shadow of National Socialism and Fascism over Europe and its legal traditions.* Oxford: Hart Publishing, 243–266.
Weir, L. (2013). Roberto Esposito's political philosophy of the gift, *Angelaki* 18(3), 155–167.
Williams, G. (1983). *Textbook of Criminal Law* (2nd Edition). London: Stevens.
Wolf, C. (2012). Before the law: Animals in a biopolitical context, *Law, Culture and the Humanities* 6(1), 8–23.
Wright, W. (2000). Historical analogies, slippery slopes, and the question of euthanasia, *The Journal of Law, Medicine & Ethics* 28(2), 176–186.
Yuill, K. (2013). *Assisted Suicide: The liberal, humanist case against legalization.* New York: Palgrave Macmillan.
Zamboni, M. (2008). The "social" in social law: An analysis of a concept in disguise, *Journal of Law in Society* 9, 63.

Index

For Product Safety Concerns and Information please contact our EU representative GPSR@taylorandfrancis.com Taylor & Francis Verlag GmbH, Kaufingerstraße 24, 80331 München, Germany